Chatham House Papers · 20

Defence and Public Opinion

Chatham House Papers · 20

Defence and Public Opinion

*David Capitanchik
and Richard C. Eichenberg*

The Royal Institute of International Affairs

Routledge & Kegan Paul
London, Boston and Henley

The Royal Institute of International Affairs is an unofficial body which promotes the scientific study of international questions and does not express opinions of its own. The opinions expressed in this paper are the responsibility of the authors.

First published 1983
by Routledge & Kegan Paul Ltd
39 Store Street, London WC1E 7DD,
9 Park Street, Boston, Mass. 02108, USA and
Broadway House, Newtown Road,
Henley-on-Thames, Oxon RG9 1EN
Set by Hope Services, Abingdon and
printed in Great Britain by
Billing and Son Ltd, Worcester
© Royal Institute of International Affairs 1983
No part of this book may be reproduced in
any form without permission from the
publisher, except for the quotation of brief
passages in criticism.

Library of Congress Cataloging in Publication Data
Capitanchik, David B. (David Bernard), 1934–
Defence and public opinion.
(Chatham House papers: 20)
Includes bibliographical references.
1. North Atlantic Treaty Organization – Public opinion.
2. Europe – Defenses – Public opinion.   3. United States –
Defenses – Public opinion.   4. Public opinion – Europe.
5 Public opinion – United States.   I. Eichenberg,
Richard, 1952–   .   II. Title.   III. Series.
UA646.3.C26 1983   355'.031'091821   83-19184
ISBN 0-7100-9356-X

Contents

Preface

Public opinion is arguably one of the most ill-defined and loosely used terms in the vocabulary of political discourse. Its assessment, until relatively recently, was largely a matter of speculation or, at best, informed hunch. In what follows, in order to gauge the state of popular opinion about defence, we have used contemporary survey data from polls conducted, in the main, by commercial polling organizations — data which, increasingly, are being deposited in archives in Europe and the United States. We have used this material in order to make comparisons — both over time and between nations — of opinion in seven of the member countries of the Atlantic Alliance.

We chose to focus upon certain Alliance members, rather than others, mainly for reasons of space. The relative abundance of data in the case of the Netherlands, and the peculiar circumstances, such as the non-nuclear policies, of the Scandinavian countries made their inclusion obvious. It would have taken a much longer book and an ideal world, in which comprehensive archives were generally available, to have covered all the Alliance members. We fully acknowledge that we have excluded other interesting cases, for example Italy, which would be an obvious candidate for inclusion in any future study.

David Capitanchik prepared Chapters 1 and 2, and the country studies on the United Kingdom, France and Scandinavia, as well as the final version of Chapter 9. Richard Eichenberg, whose collaboration was vital to the entire project, prepared the country studies on the United States, West Germany and the Netherlands, and contributed important overall observations which are incorporated in Chapter 9.

This paper forms part of a wider Chatham House research project on US foreign policy and European interests which has been funded by the Leverhulme Trust. Eichenberg's research was accomplished as part of a larger project, 'Wealth, Welfare and Security', prepared with Catherine McArdle Kelleher and William Domke. The project was supported by a generous grant from the Ford Foundation. Time for writing was provided by the Policy Sciences Program at Florida State University.

The collection of survey materials could not have been completed without the assistance of numerous individuals and institutions. Eichenberg would like to single out Connie de Boers of the POLLS Archive, University of Amsterdam, who was both hospitable and helpful in searching the unique holdings of the archive. Dutch hospitality was also extended by the Netherlands Institute for Studies on Peace and Security (Clingendael), the Netherlands Institute for Public Opinion, and the Steinmetz Archive. In the Hague, he benefited from conversations with Dr Jan Siccama, Dr Philip Everts and Dr Jan Stapel. In West Germany, he was lucky to have the help of Maria Wieken-Mayser, who guided him to sources elsewhere in Europe. His colleague Russ Dalton at Florida State has been very helpful in locating and interpreting surveys. Yvonne Addy Zweede provided excellent translations of the Dutch polls. Public opinion polling has for some time been a common task of European ministries involved in foreign affairs. Officials in both the Netherlands and West Germany were most helpful in interpreting their surveys. American agencies have also been helpful: the United States Information Agency shared the results of their European surveys and the Department of State provided results from their collection of American polls.

Capitanchik wishes to express particular gratitude to Kathy Sayer of the SSRC Data Archive at Essex University, to Nadia Déhan at the Centre d'Etude de la Vie Politique Française Contemporaine, Paris, to the Norwegian Social Science Data Services in Bergen and to the Danish Data Archives at the University of Odense.

Both authors are indebted to Professor Lawrence Freedman of King's College, London, and to Joan Pearce and Pauline Wickham of Chatham House. Last, but by no means least, they wish to thank their

devoted secretaries in Aberdeen and Tallahasse, and also their families
— all of whom put up with their demands with typical calm and sanity.

D.C.
R.C.E.

1 Introduction

The Atlantic Alliance is passing through a period in which its unity and cohesion are perceived as being under great strain. The purpose of this paper is to examine one of the major causes of the current anxiety about the Alliance's future, namely the climate of opinion about defence. Popular public opinion, with its overriding preoccupation with immediate economic and social problems, has tended to acquiesce in or be largely indifferent towards national security affairs. Now, it is believed, support for the Alliance is threatened by the strains of world recession, the apparent disunity among policy elites and the re-emergence of protest movements. This paper seeks to examine this assumption by reference to the evidence of public opinion surveys.

Over the years the problems of the Alliance and the internal controversies that they have caused have been widely aired both at the official level and in the media. The immediate causes of any quarrel, whether the acquisition of a new weapons system or, frequently, the Alliance's reaction to some international crisis, have tended to turn quickly into debates about fundamental issues. These have included the nature and extent of the Soviet threat and how far the allies have been prepared to share the burden of meeting it; the degree and consequences of the Europeans' dependence on the United States for their security; and the ability, not to say willingness, of America's partners to reduce this reliance.[1]

France has long asserted its independence of the transatlantic connection by withdrawing from NATO's joint military command and developing an autonomous nuclear defence capability. The United Kingdom, by contrast, has chosen to play a principal role in the Alliance,

1

basing its security largely on the so-called 'special relationship' with the United States. This has involved depending on the Americans for much of the research and development, as well as components, of its 'independent nuclear deterrent'. For their part, the Scandinavian members of the Alliance have rejected the location of foreign bases on their territory and have shunned direct contact with nuclear weapons. And yet, in the face of such diversity, the Alliance has survived.

In the 1980s, however, two developments have threatened its cohesion. First, the world recession has exacerbated competition among the allies and has inclined governments to pursue narrowly self-interested economic policies, making it difficult to preserve Alliance solidarity. The security relationship among Western states, it is feared, might also suffer in a climate of hostility and resentment fostered by competition for scarce markets and jobs and disappointed expectations of continued high and secure living standards.

Second, the flourishing public debate over defence has seemed to threaten the security relationship which lies at the heart of the Atlantic Alliance. Protest movements have existed for a quarter of a century. They appear now to be undermining the broad public acceptance of the doctrines of the few who make policy. Opposition to the nature and deployment of nuclear weapons unites what is a very loose coalition of individuals, groups and organizations.[2] But it is related to broader pacifist tendencies and, above all, to a neutralism which could, it is sometimes suggested, weaken if not destroy the Alliance.

Public opinion has been sensitive also to the differences of view evident among policy elites. The controversy over Intermediate Nuclear Forces (INF) is a case in point, but there have also been arguments between the Europeans and the Americans over, among other things, the Siberian gas pipeline, sanctions against Poland, steel imports into the United States, the sale of surplus EEC agricultural produce and, importantly, levels of defence spending. Within the various member countries, divisions have emerged, to be seized upon by the dissenters as evidence not only of disarray among policy-makers, but of the existence of support in the most influential circles for their point of view:[3] all this in addition to the regular cleavages between political parties and disagreements within them.[4] Small wonder, then, if the public reaction to official policy were to be less acquiescent and more questioning than in the past.

In the course of what follows, we shall be looking at where public opinion actually stands in the national opinion surveys of key Alliance partners and the extent to which any visible shifts have occurred. Frequent reference is made to recent events in the defence field which, in addition to the longer-term factors, have had a significant short-term impact on opinion. Similarly, concepts such as deterrence are referred to throughout the paper. It is therefore worth outlining some of the ideas and events that have dominated defence thinking in the recent period.

The Atlantic Alliance has always been based upon the commitment of American power to helping the West Europeans defend themselves by means of a system of 'extended nuclear deterrence'. The object of deterrence is to persuade an adversary that the costs of him seeking a military solution to political differences will exceed by far any benefits. The West Europeans have found reliance on their belief in the supremacy of American nuclear forces over those of the Soviet Union a cheap solution to their defence problems and an adequate substitute for having to provide for their own security. It is sometimes suggested that one of the main reasons for the rise in the 1980s of the peace movement in Europe, with its corresponding anti-Americanism (and, for that matter, the rise of the peace movement in the United States), is the emergence of nuclear parity between the superpowers, which has led many people to perceive nuclear war as a far greater threat to the future of mankind than Soviet aggression. Moreover, even among those who are concerned about the Soviet threat to the West, there are many who argue for a reduction in the reliance on the nuclear component of deterrence; and there have been calls from within influential European opinion for Europe to be more self-sufficient in its non-nuclear defence.[5]

It is against this background that public opinion about nuclear deterrence needs to be evaluated. Undoubtedly, it was reflected in the debate raging through the Alliance in the early months of 1983 over INF.[6] In West Germany, where the majority of public opinion supports NATO membership and favours Alliance policies in general, a majority has also opposed the deployment of new theatre nuclear weapons. A similar phenomenon has existed in the United Kingdom. Elsewhere in Europe even the most conservative governments, such as that of Belgium, have adopted a policy of wait-and-see regarding their commitment to the INF deployment. What became known as the dual-track decision, which was designed to boost the credibility of the US nuclear umbrella, has been subject to a shift of emphasis. In the mid-1970s, European fears that superpower parity in strategic weapons might make the Americans reluctant to intervene if the Soviets limited a war to Europe, resulted in a decision in December 1979 to deploy new intermediate range missiles in the European theatre. An American offer to the Europeans of joint firing arrangements was rejected at the time, partly because of cost, but mainly because it was thought that the US commitment to Europe would be more convincing to the Russians if the new missiles were wholly American-owned and American-operated. At the same time, to allay public concern, the NATO Ministerial Council decided that the United States should seek to negotiate with the USSR for the limitation of all intermediate nuclear forces in the European theatre.

Now things seem to have changed. European pressures on the United States are all in the direction of reducing, rather than increasing, its nuclear weaponry in general and in Europe in particular. Cruise and Pershing missiles are now regarded less as bargaining counters. There are widespread demands for them not to be deployed at all even if the Soviets fail to remove their SS-20s from the Western front. In Europe, lack of public confidence in the United States already seems to have had the effect of changing attitudes of many among the policy elites. In contrast to the mid-1970s, they are now demanding, or at least examining, the feasibility of some dual firing arrangement if the new missiles are deployed, in order to reassure worried public opinion.

A similar public outcry in Europe greeted the attempt by the Carter administration, in 1977-8, to strengthen European defences by deploying enhanced radiation warheads, the so-called 'neutron bombs', on European soil. To the Europeans, this seemed to suggest that the Americans might actually be prepared to fight a nuclear war in Europe and, like INF, was regarded as an attempt by the United States to impose unwanted nuclear weapons on Europe. Unlike the case of cruise and Pershing II missiles, President Carter cancelled the neutron warhead programme, although it has recently been revived by the Reagan administration.

Paradoxically, then, the cohesion of the Alliance has frequently been threatened in recent times by attempts to strengthen the West's capacity to deter any Soviet military threat. In 1978, an agreement to increase the defence budgets of Alliance countries by a steady 3% per annum (in real terms) caused friction between the parties (who have varied in honouring the agreement) rather than enhancing the deterrent.

Differences have also been evident among the allies over a range of political and economic issues stemming from the global role of the United States; the particular interests of the EEC and the individual European countries; and different perceptions of Soviet intentions and motivations. Nowhere has this been more evident than in the Middle East and the Persian Gulf. The failure of the NATO powers to support US policy during the October 1973 war brought into the open some profound differences between the Americans and the Europeans over the Arab-Israeli conflict. The American proposal for a Rapid Deployment Force (RDF), designed to intervene in the event of a threat to vital Western interests in the Arabian Gulf, has also caused difficulties for the Alliance. It would divert US forces from Europe at a time when there was likely to be a more general confrontation with the Soviet Union, and it would require European participation, or at least agreement, in order to be palatable to American public opinion when, in fact, there is no agreement between the Americans and their allies over attitudes towards the Arab world.

Finally, since December 1979, when the Soviet Union invaded Afghanistan, differences — at times acrimonious — have arisen between the United States and its European partners over the appropriate Western response. The tendency of the Europeans to see the Soviet regime as the successor to that of the Tsars — impelled by national ambition, by its desire for security and the maintenance of its empire — conflicts with an American view which regards the Soviets as having embarked upon an ideological campaign to create a communist world and therefore as not being susceptible to containment. The Europeans' reaction to the Polish crisis of 1980-1 was consequently different from that of the Americans. American insistence on embargoes, and on other measures designed to weaken and eventually disintegrate the Soviet world, conflicts with the European view that everything should be done to give the Soviet Union a firm stake in maintaining the *status quo* and not embarking upon military adventures.

Against this background, there has been growing concern that the enhanced visibility of the issues, as they are aired in the mass media and discussed and commented upon by academics and other experts, might lead to shifts in public opinion. In particular, officials fear and critics hope that the various peace movements and their much publicized activities have in fact swayed popular opinion away from passive support for Alliance policies to active hostility towards them.

It is not the purpose of this paper to consider in any detail whether or how public opinion influences policy. Suffice it to say that it does to the extent, at least, that debates among policy elites are in many cases conducted on the basis of assumptions about the state of public opinion. For this reason alone, it is necessary to investigate whether public opinion about defence has changed in recent years or is in the process of doing so.

The paper starts out, in Chapter 2, by discussing the concept and measurement of public opinion. Too often, references to 'public opinion' are confused by a lack of clarity about a very loosely defined term. Chapters 3–8 deal with individual countries. In each case, several aspects of public opinion are examined: the priority given to defence questions; attitudes towards defence spending; views on nuclear weapons; disposition towards the United States and NATO. Chapter 9 draws some overall conclusions about the extent to which public opinion on defence policy has changed or shifted and the significance of these shifts.

2 Public Opinion

It is important at the outset to distinguish between the public 'in general' and specialist or 'attentive' publics, bodies within and outside official circles whose opinions 'governments might find it prudent to heed'.[1] In most issue areas, there are those who make it their business to inform themselves about certain matters, such as defence, because they have some vested or personal interest in them and because they want to bring pressure to bear on policy. But there is also the mass public for whom defence, the environment, animal welfare or women's rights are not matters of everyday concern.

What this mass public thinks and feels about political issues has been of interest only since universal adult suffrage became the essence of what, in the West, is meant by democracy. Direct democracy, in which all citizens actively participate in governing the affairs of their communities, has never been possible in practice except in very small units, and the advent of mass industrial society has rendered the idea of direct popular participation in the policy-making process virtually meaningless. The modern polity has been characterized by indirect representative democracy, which in effect has meant the continuation, as in the past, of rule by relatively small elites. The difference is that nowadays, in the liberal Western state, elites claim to be representative in the sense that they have been chosen by their citizens at fairly regular intervals. The emergence of the mass electorate has made 'what the public thinks' in general, but also on particular issues, a matter of importance. What influences electoral choice is of major concern to politicians and all involved in the making of policy.

Until the introduction of public opinion polls, the views of the public could be ascertained only indirectly through such channels as demonstrations, strikes and petitions. In Britain the march of the Jarrow unemployed in the 1930s and the reception they received en route, the ex-servicemen's demonstrations in the United States during the same world recession, the mass demonstrations and rioting leading up to the assumption of power by the Nazis in pre-war Germany, were expressions of public opinion, albeit organized in one form or another. Apart from such manifestations, there were elections and the occasional plebiscite or referendum, sometimes conducted by governments, but also by bodies independent of the authorities. In Britain, in 1935, for example, the League of Nations Union held a famous Peace Ballot which has been described by one historian of the period as 'a sort of pioneer Gallup Poll on a huge scale'.[2] It showed that not only did the public support the League (11 million voted in favour of it), but that by a majority of 3:1 it was in favour of backing it up with military action. But it is important to emphasize that such evidence of mass public opinion could not claim to have scientific validity. Questions could be framed so as to produce desired answers and the results themselves rigged so as to create the most favourable impression.

Different conceptions of public opinion

There is, first, a body of unorganized opinion which consists of the soundings made by civil servants, ministers and parliamentarians as they go about their daily business in government, in the legislature and among their constituents. This is often described as 'public opinion' and, since it is experienced directly by those who are involved in the making of policy, it is bound to be highly influential.

The term 'public opinion' is used also in describing the activities of pressure groups. Some of these campaign openly for support; others content themselves with unobtrusive lobbying. In the case of defence, a number of groups have emerged in the past few years, to operate at various levels and to employ a variety of techniques to promote their cause. The Campaign for Nuclear Disarmament in the United Kingdom and its affiliates on the Continent in END are well-known examples. In West Germany, the so-called Green Party has been active in the anti-nuclear lobby, and in the Netherlands, it is reported, the

Interchurch Peace Council has joined with the communist-led Stop De N-Bom movement to form an umbrella group for about 400 different pacifist organizations. In Scandinavia, the Women for Peace movement claims to have a massive membership and, together with a Norwegian group called No To Atomic Weapons, is advocating a Scandinavian nuclear-free zone.[3] The opposing view is represented by more conservative political groupings, whose aim is to promote greater public support for current Alliance defence doctrines and, in some cases, to urge governments to enhance, rather than reduce, their military capabilities.[4]

Some would argue that the influence of these groups has been considerable, both directly in affecting policy and indirectly in moulding public attitudes. Their impact can be assessed only indirectly – by looking at support for or opposition to the causes they espouse. There can be little doubt that they generate a great deal of information and debate, but it is not easy to isolate their particular impact from other influences upon public opinion and policy. Their influence upon policy, however, is likely to be greater than that of the general public because they are articulate and organized.

Similar statements could be made about the impact of political parties and academic groups. Together they constitute the informed and interested public that holds opinions about defence and seeks to influence, either by propaganda or by academic argument, those who make policy as well as those whose general support the policy-makers require. Through the mass media they communicate their ideas to the general public and seek to influence the 'public opinion' with which this study is primarily concerned.

Public opinion, 'in the sense of the opinion of the whole public, i.e. all adults or all electors, is amorphous, unchannelled and has no means of communication open to it except by voting . . . The opinion poll has emerged as a means of communicating the unformulated opinion of a mass electorate so that the opinions of special publics can be set in a wider context.'[5] It has been suggested that public opinion on any matter when one is referring to the 'public at large' or 'public in general', as opposed to particular 'publics', is 'the hypothetical result of an imaginary plebiscite thereon'.[6] Its importance lies in the effect it is likely to have on voting when those responsible for the conduct of the nation's affairs next present themselves for re-election.

Public opinion

The idea of public opinion as the expression of what the population in general thinks about any issue of political significance has always been of interest. The advent of scientific opinion polling has made it possible to elicit information, in a formal rather than an amorphous manner, about what the mass public actually does think.

Opinion polls

The bulk of the data upon which this book is based is derived from the published results of commercial polling organizations. Among these are the various national affiliates of the Gallup Poll. This is not because we regard these polls as more reliable than many others conducted by similar reputable concerns. Rather, it is because Gallup Polls are published on a regular basis and, even when not specifically commissioned by clients, include questions relevant to this study. Each national Gallup organization is autonomous, but they all ask similar questions and participate in international polls, such as the 'End-of-Year Poll Results' published by Gallup International Research Institutes Inc., which make straight cross-national comparisons of trends in public opinion possible. In the United States, considerably more polling organizations exist than in Europe. For purposes of comparability, we have relied largely on surveys published by the United States International Communications Agency, which is a governmental body that draws upon surveys conducted by organizations including Gallup for its data.

The reliability of opinion polls, and hence confidence in their being a fair reflection of what the public in general thinks, depend upon three main factors. First, and possibly foremost, is the structure of the questionnaire and the nature of the questions that it asks. So far as the structure is concerned, the sequence of the questions is important, and particular attention has to be paid that the topics raised are not 'such as to contaminate the answers to subsequent questions by the introduction of ideas such as fears of disagreeable consequences in earlier questions'.[7] Questions must be phrased so as to be clearly understood by those with the lowest intelligence and education. This is particularly important when they are directed at a representative sample of the population, which will, one hopes, include about the same percentage of illiterates (approximately 5% in the UK) and those with a reading age of, say, below twelve years (about 10% in the UK) as is to be found in the population as a whole.[8] Questions must obviously be as unambiguous and as free from bias as one can make them. The degree of reliability of polls clearly depends upon questions being intelligible, neutral and, further, of some relevance to the experience or interest of the persons interviewed. It is for this reason that polls which ask questions on specific issues such as defence try to find out the priorities given by the public to national political issues. Such questions as 'What do you think is the single most urgent problem facing Great Britain today?' (NOP) or 'What would you say is the most urgent problem facing the country at the present time?' (Gallup) are a necessary prerequisite of any investigation of public opinion about a specific issue and provide the context within which the answers to issue questions can be evaluated. The same needs to be asked about the public's knowledge of the issues. Are ill-informed opinions of any relevance or value? There can be little argument that opinions based upon ignorance are of very limited value in determining policy, but they can well be a vital guide in determining its implementation and presentation. This would be true in relation to most matters, but it is particularly true of defence affairs, where it is essential for governments and those responsible for decision-making, as well as those who try to analyse the public's reponse to policy decisions, to know what the public thinks, however ill-conceived and poorly informed its opinion may be.

The second factor is the professionalism of the interviewers. Gaining the confidence and cooperation of interviewees is essential, as is thoroughgoing conscientiousness in completing the questionnaires. It is an aspect of polling that is so fundamental that it must be at the forefront of the concerns of any professional commercial polling organization if it is to have any credibility.

Third and last, there is the matter of sampling. If opinion polls are viewed with suspicion, if doubt is cast upon their findings, if even the most informed and attentive publics dispute their validity, then it is due largely to disbelief that 1,000 interviewees can ever really reflect the opinions of tens of millions of their fellow citizens. But what really matters is how the sample is constructed and selected.[9]

11

Sampling is used widely in science and medicine, as well as in industry as a quality control, but there are obviously special problems in sampling human populations. Suffice it to say, here, that proof of its validity can be seen in many instances, not least in the remarkable accuracy of the major opinion polls when it comes to the prediction, say, of election results (see Table 1).

It is important to emphasize, as Webb and Wybrow do in their writings on the subject, that the size of the sample used is a vital factor in determining the accuracy of polls, but *not* the size of the population from which the sample is derived. It is scientifically correct, whatever people may feel, that 1,000 interviews in, say, Aberdeen will produce results of equal validity for Aberdeen, provided all the rules of sampling have been observed, as a sample of the same size would for the population of the United Kingdom as a whole.

The other point to be borne in mind is that polls using a sample of 1,000–2,000 respondents, as most of the national polls quoted here do, can be expected to be accurate within a margin of error of ±3%. Such an error would be important in attempting to predict the outcome of a close election; it is less significant when it comes to surveys of public opinion on issues such as those with which this study is concerned.

Thus public opinion, as the term is used in the following chapters, consists of the opinions expressed about defence and related issues by a scientifically selected sample of the adult populations of the United States and European members of the Atlantic Alliance. These opinions have been derived in the main from the findings of surveys conducted by commercial polling organizations.

In the past, in none of the countries treated in this study has the mass public appeared to assign to defence a very high priority among its concerns. Defence policy in general seems to have been an issue which people have preferred to leave to the discretion of their governments. Various aspects of defence are, however, more controversial: nuclear weapons policy and deployment, defence expenditures and Alliance relations are cases in point. But just how far public opinion has reflected, influenced or been influenced by the crises that have bedevilled NATO remains to be seen. The chapters that follow comprise descriptions of the state of public opinion about national security

Table 1   Gallup's election record, 1945–79 (%)

General election	Gallup final survey	Election result[a]	Error on major party
1945	47.0 Labour	49.0 Labour	−2.0 Labour
1950[b]	45.0 Labour	46.8 Labour	−1.8 Labour
1951	49.5 Conservative	49.3 Labour	−2.2 Labour
1955	51.0 Conservative	49.3 Conservative	+1.7 Conservative
1959	49.5 Conservative	48.8 Conservative	+0.7 Conservative
1964	46.5 Labour	44.8 Labour	+1.7 Labour
1966	51.0 Labour	48.9 Labour	+2.1 Labour
1970[c]	49.0 Labour	46.2 Conservative	−4.2 Conservative
1974 Feb.[d]	39.5 Conservative	38.6 Conservative	+0.9 Conservative
1974 Oct.	41.5 Labour	40.2 Labour	+1.3 Labour
1979	43.0 Conservative	44.9 Conservative	−1.9 Conservative
1975 EEC referendum:			
'Yes' percentage	68.0	67.5	+0.5
Turnout percentage	65.0	64.5	+0.5
1979 European parliament election:	51.0 Conservative	50.6 Conservative	+0.4 Conservative

a The figure shown is the percentage of the party with the largest share of the vote; it is not always the party that formed the government.
b The Labour Party obtained the largest share of the votes, but did not do so in terms of seats. The Conservative Party, therefore, became the new government.
c The final report said Labour would win; the Conservatives narrowly won.
d The final report said the Conservative Party would obtain the largest share of the votes – it did so. It did not, however, obtain the overall majority of the seats and a minority Labour government was formed.

in the United States and among its NATO allies, wherever possible in the context of what importance the public attaches to defence and its knowledge of what is involved.

In the case of most issues, such evidence as does exist reveals a remarkable consistency in public opinion, with the only deviations from long-term trends coinciding with dramatic international events, including the Soviet invasions of Czechoslovakia and Afghanistan and the Falklands crisis. Deep divisions among policy elites as reflected in the media, such as the debate in the United Kingdom over Britain's nuclear modernization programme (Trident D5), the MX missile debate in the United States and the INF issue across Europe, have also been reflected in the state of public opinion.

Public opinion, in the broadest popular sense of the term, seems to follow elite opinion rather than vice versa. As we shall show, in every country of the Alliance the majority supports the broad lines of official defence policy. There is a widespread revulsion against the deployment of certain types of nuclear weapons, and in some cases, for example in the United Kingdom, there is support for weapons that are independently owned and controlled, rather than UK-based American nuclear forces — an attitude that possibly reflects strains in relations between Europe and the United States.

In the chapters that follow, we hope to be able to ascertain to what extent any marked changes have occurred in public support for the Alliance and its policies. We shall examine the degree to which expressions of concern about the future of the Alliance because of failing public support are justified. We shall also have regard to the extent to which policy-makers can still count on support for any policy they deem necessary. As we pass from country to country, we shall attempt to make broad comparisons between public attitudes so as to gain some picture of Alliance cohesion at the public level. And, above all, we hope to be able to provide evidence of a more substantial nature than has been available hitherto about the state of public opinion in the Alliance.

3 The United Kingdom

The British people have consistently assigned to defence a relatively low position in their scale of national priorities. Only in 1983 did it figure prominently as an election issue. Otherwise, issues of direct relevance such as unemployment, inflation, industrial relations and other economic problems have always figured larger.

Recently, however, the country's defence effort has been the object of attention and controversy to an extent unknown for at least two decades. Traditionally, the disposition of the British public has been to go along with whatever defence policies governments have deemed desirable. Now, it is argued, changes are taking place. There has been the revival of the Campaign for Nuclear Disarmament (CND), with unilateralism again an issue in the conflict among the various factions in the Labour Party, as it was in the early 1960s, except that this time the issue has been resolved by the official adoption of a unilateralist policy. The nuclear issue also divides the generations, with consequences for the defence policies of the parties in the centre of the British political spectrum. At the Liberal Assembly in Llandudno in 1981, for example, the Young Liberals won a commitment for the Party to campaign against the siting of cruise missiles in Britain, which also said that the United Kingdom should take the initiative in calling for a European nuclear-free zone.

The nuclear debate has found its echo in public opinion as reflected in the polls. Although there has been controversy over Britain's nuclear modernization plans, public opinion seems to have been disturbed most by US policy. While still supporting NATO, it exhibits considerable concern about American leadership of the Alliance. In common

15

with other countries in Europe, a sizeable proportion of the population seems to feel that 'far from the Americans being in Europe to help the West Europeans defend themselves, they are here in order to prosecute "their" war – a war in which the Europeans have no interest and from which they will be the first to suffer.'[1]

Perceptions of the threat

Gallup introduced its first 'End-of-Year Poll' in 1957. Since then, the British public, in answer to questions about its expectations for the immediate future ('Which of these do you think is likely to be true of the coming year?'), has been consistently pessimistic about the prospects for international peace. In only two years out of the past twenty-five, in 1959 and 1963, were people more optimistic than pessimistic about the future. Perhaps it is significant that 1963 was the year of the signing of the Partial Nuclear Test Ban Treaty, which not only seemed to herald a more peaceful era in international relations, but also allayed public concern that arose in the mid-1950s about health hazards emanating from nuclear tests in the atmosphere. Generally, the trends of public opinion have been steady, with any variation coinciding with dramatic international events. Since 1971, however, with the exception of the year in which the late President Sadat made his historic visit to Jerusalem (1977), opinion has become steadily more pessimistic, with never less than twice, and in one year (1979) as much as ten times, as many believing that the following year would be troubled as believed that it would be peaceful.

The polls also show that nearly two-thirds of respondents have been prepared to express an opinion about Soviet power and whether it is likely to increase. Of these, rarely less than four times as many have consistently stated their belief that Soviet power in the world would increase as those believing it would decline. A somewhat smaller majority has believed that the United States would increase its power (see Table 2).

About three-quarters of respondents to opinion polls have a 'somewhat or very unfavourable' opinion of the USSR. A similar proportion also believes that Soviet overtures towards the West should be treated with suspicion. A clear majority, around 60%, has believed that the

Table 2   End-of-Year Poll: British trends (%)
Q: 'Which of these do you think is likely to be true of 19 . . [the next year]?'

	1959	1961	1963	1965	1967	1969	1971	1973	1975	1977	1979	1981
Peaceful; more or less free of international disputes	52	13	47	18	24	34	16	20	26	33	7	15
Troubled with much international discord	21	56	20	59	43	39	61	61	53	33	69	55
No opinion	27	31	33	23	33	27	23	18	21	34	24	29
Russia will increase its power in the world	46	45	40	40	48	43	39	35	44	39	41	36
Russian power will decline	16	14	17	20	12	15	13	13	12	9	6	13
No opinion; stay same	38	41	43	40	40	42	48	52	44	53	54	50
America will increase its power in the world	39	39	43	47	38	44	29	24	30	30	35	43
American power will decline	21	16	16	17	25	21	28	34	27	16	19	11
No opinion; stay same	40	45	41	36	37	35	43	42	43	54	45	46

Source: Gallup Political Index, Report No. 268.

Soviet Union poses a threat to Britain in the scientific and political fields, whereas consistently below 50% have seen it as threatening Britain's economy.[2]

As is to be expected, it is in the military field that the Soviet threat looms largest. Depending upon the circumstances of the times, not less than 60% of respondents have regarded the Soviet Union as posing a military threat to Britain, while never more than 20% have believed it to present no threat at all. At the time of the invasion of Afghanistan, as many as 85% saw it as a threat to the United Kingdom in the military field, and as recently as March 1982 some 75% thought that it would be better to fight than to accept Russian domination, regardless of how horrible a modern war would inevitably be.[3]

On the subject of war, and in particular the possibility of a world-wide war breaking out in which nuclear weapons would be used, public opinion is significantly more pessimistic today than it was twenty years ago. In a poll conducted in January 1983, over 60% said they were worried about such a war breaking out as compared with barely 40% in 1964.[4] Recently, also, the percentage of those who have thought that such a war would occur within the next ten years has increased. In the wake of the Soviet incursion into Afghanistan, one poll showed that as many as 40% of respondents believed that there would be a world war within the next ten years.[5] Indeed, since the end of the 1970s, the public generally has become less sanguine about the prospects for peace and the orderly conduct of international affairs.

When questioned on specific aspects of defence and on perceptions of the threat to the nation's security in particular, changes which may prove to be of considerable significance have appeared over recent years. However, it is important to note that little more than one adult in twenty reckons defence and international affairs among the top issues facing the country. With the exception of questions relating largely to the current nuclear controversies, the majority of public opinion has tended to go along with whatever the government of the day has deemed necessary for defence. Indeed, there has been consistent and widespread support for whatever allocation of the nation's resources the authorities have decided to make to defence.

Defence expenditure

All the major public opinion polls show with monotonous regularity the high priority that the public assigns to economic issues above all other national affairs. For their part, all administrations for the past quarter of a century have faced budgetary difficulties, particularly as they grappled with defence policy; and competing demands for limited resources have constituted the main domestic restraint on policy decisions.[6] Nevertheless, in respect of defence spending, British public opinion has been remarkably stable. During the five-year period from 1977 to 1982, in response to questions about public expenditure, those replying that spending on armaments and defence was either too little or about right have been consistently within ±3 of 60%.[7] Only a quarter of respondents at most have thought that too much was being spent on defence. In July 1982, in the wake of the Falklands war, 40% thought that government spending on defence was too little, and a further 25% said it was about right.[8]

It is true, of course, as the same July 1982 poll showed, that the public would like more to be spent on most things. Thus, for example, 70% wanted more to be spent on education and health, and 66% thought spending on pensions was too low. Moreover, the absence of what the pollsters call 'trade-off' questions makes it difficult to assess whether and to what extent people would be prepared to forgo expenditure on education, health or pensions in order to sustain or increase defence allocations. However, in a poll conducted for *The Economist* on 21-23 June 1982, 71% said that 'retaining sovereignty [of the Falklands] was important enough to pay increased taxes to maintain the military forces to protect the islands'.[9]

None the less, it is important to distinguish between the public's view of the size and even purpose of the nation's defence effort and its view of its content or nature. In the United Kingdom, as would be the case throughout NATO, the defence of the country's territorial integrity· is regarded as an unquestionable duty and, as was seen in the South Atlantic, what constitutes a nation's territory can be construed very widely indeed. The defence of the nation seems to include the defence of its citizens, its national pride, its economic interests, as well as even broader matters. The management of defence is included in the public's estimate of how well the government is handling the nation's affairs in general. The content of the defence effort is another matter, however, especially its nuclear dimension.

The nuclear deterrent

The revival of interest in security issues in Western Europe and Scandinavia is exemplified by the re-emergence of the anti-nuclear movements which had flourished in the 1950s. The campaigners have embraced a broad spectrum of groups, including, for example, the ecology and feminist movements. Some are opposed to nuclear power and even nuclear research for any purpose, while others support improvements in NATO's conventional military capability, which they regard as being endangered by expensive government programmes for the replacement of obsolescent existing nuclear weapon systems. Widespread opposition to nuclear weapons is to be found also within one of the pillars of the British establishment, namely the Church of England. At a meeting in February 1983, the General Synod rejected a call for unilateral nuclear disarmament that had been included in a specially commissioned report on 'The Church and the Bomb', but at the same time it asked the government to commit itself to a policy of 'no first use of nuclear weapons'.[10]

Meanwhile, the government remains committed to the stationing of 160 cruise missiles in southern England, and their deployment is due to begin by the end of 1983. This is in addition to its decision, announced in March 1982, to proceed with the replacement of Britain's ageing Polaris fleet with the Trident-2(D5) system, at a cost of anything up to £10,000 billion at present prices, in order to maintain the independent nuclear deterrent.

The general public is not as ill-informed about these matters as is often imagined. There seems to be a widespread and reasonably accurate knowledge, for example, of what the media insist on calling the neutron 'bomb'. In May 1978, 78% had heard or read about it, and in another poll, in September 1981, 81% knew of its existence. Moreover, roughly two-thirds of respondents had a basic awareness of how it differed from other nuclear devices.[11] In August 1980, another poll showed that 81% of respondents had heard of NATO, although only 29% were able to say accurately what the initials stood for. Nevertheless, it cannot be said that the public has anything like the extent of knowledge about defence that would enable it to contribute directly to the making of policy. As we stated earlier, however, so far as politics are concerned, what matters is what the public believes or feels or thinks, rather than what it knows.

On average, over the past two decades, virtually two-thirds of the population have believed that it is best for Britain's security to have nuclear weapons. The proportion rose slightly in the wake of the Soviet invasion of Afghanistan and went up to 67% in January 1980. Nearly two years later, when not only had the impact of Afghanistan receded, but concern was most intense about the Reagan administration's military policies, the stationing of US missiles in Europe, the neutron device and Britain's Trident programme, and when the activities of the anti-nuclear protestors and debates about nuclear policy were receiving greater publicity than for many years past, 58% still believed that it would be a bad idea for Britain to give up its reliance on nuclear weapons for its security. At that time, 33% of those asked replied that they were in favour of abandoning reliance on nuclear weapons even if other countries decided to keep them. While this represented an increase of some 12% on the previous year, it is still well below the percentage that supported unilateralism in the early 1960s.[12] But the situation is shifting. Since the early months of 1982, there has been a steady trend away from support for unilateral nuclear disarmament. Thus, in January 1983, 65% thought it would be a mistake for Britain to give up relying on nuclear weapons for defence.[13]

On the other hand, over the past twenty years, people have become more concerned about nuclear weapons and the likelihood of nuclear war breaking out. In April 1963, when Gallup first asked about the likelihood of there ever being a nuclear war, only 16% thought that it could happen, while 59% thought not. It is perhaps some measure of increasing public pessimism that, in answer to the same question in January 1983, 61% were worried about the chances of a world war breaking out in which nuclear bombs would be used, as opposed to only 38% who had no such fears. In 1980, 39% of respondents to a poll question replied that they thought it was likely that a nuclear war would occur one day, and 45% thought that it was not. In January

21

1983, these proportions were reversed, with 49% thinking a nuclear war was likely and only 39% disagreeing.[14]

One poll has suggested that there are considerable variations in responses to these questions according to age and class. Those under 25 years of age are roughly twice as likely to believe in the possibility of nuclear war than those over 65, and middle-class people seem to expect a war more than the working classes.[15] As one would expect, there is solid support for current defence policies among Conservative voters and supporters. The response among Labour supporters is more interesting: only 43% support the Party's policy on unilateral nuclear disarmament, while 49% believe that Britain should continue to rely on nuclear weapons for its defence.[16]

One of the most persistent claims of the nuclear disarmers has been that British possession of nuclear weapons not only would fail to deter any possible aggressor, but would actually increase the risk of the United Kingdom becoming a prime target in any future atomic war. Arguments about this question have been aired extensively in the media and have been linked with the deployment, in the United Kingdom, of new American intermediate-range missiles. Public reaction to this question, therefore, is not without significance. There has, in fact, been some increase in concern: those who believe that the stationing of nuclear weapons in Britain has increased its vulnerability to nuclear attack have risen from 26% in August 1980 to 35% in January 1983; those who think it has decreased the risk have also risen, from 37% in August 1980 to 41% in January 1983; and 24% now believe that it has no effect either way or simply have no opinion on the matter.[17]

It would seem that the extent of support for Britain's reliance on nuclear weapons for defence has changed little over the years. For most people, nuclear disarmament seems to mean multilateral rather than the unilateral abandonment of nuclear arms, regardless of whether other countries retain them. One of the reasons for this consistency is that the Warsaw Pact countries are perceived as being ahead of the West, not only in nuclear weapons but, above all, in conventional forces. Moreover, the perceived relative strengths of NATO and the Eastern bloc have hardly changed in the past three years. There is also the feeling that nuclear weapons exist, and that there is little that can be done about them. This is not inconsistent with support for attempts to negotiate arms control and disarmament agreements with the Soviet Union. But there remains only minority public support for a unilateral reduction or limitations on Britain's own independent deterrent in advance of any agreement.

Where majority public opinion does seem to diverge from official policy is in its opposition to the siting of the new American-controlled cruise missiles in Britain. There is also the finding of the polls that over the years something between a quarter and a third of the population has regularly exhibited a degree of distrust or lack of confidence in the United States. Whether this reflects an underlying anti-Americanism among the public at large is difficult to say. However, it is interesting to see public opposition to the deployment of American missiles in Britain alongside a significant current of opinion that favours Britain remaining neutral in any future global conflict.

Attitudes towards the Alliance

For many years now, over 50% of the respondents in any opinion poll have regularly expressed little or no confidence in the ability of the United States to deal wisely with current world problems. This startling finding has become even more significant in recent polls, with one, in January 1983, showing as many as 70% of those asked expressing little or no confidence in the United States compared with only 24% showing considerable or great confidence.[18]

However, this seems to have little to do with trust in Britain's principal ally to come to its aid in time of war. Between 1975 and April 1983, those expressing a great deal of trust in the United States should war break out went up from 45% to 62%.[19] Moreover, the United States has been ranked third in the polls, after the old Commonwealth countries of Canada and Australia, among a long list of allies which Britain should assist by sending troops if they were attacked by communist-backed forces. Finally, in a recent poll, the largest single percentage by far, 37%, favoured Britain providing for its security in the 1980s by remaining in NATO, among the countries of Western Europe and the United States and Canada; only 5% supported withdrawal from NATO's integrated military command; and a further 5% wanted the United Kingdom to reduce its reliance on military defence and to aim instead at greater accommodation with Russia. Of the remainder, 20% wanted a European force allied to the USA but under European command, and 21% wanted either European or national defence forces independent of the United States.[20] All in all, there is evidence to suggest that the British people would prefer to be self-reliant, rather than depend upon others for their defence. This is apparent in the support for Britain's independent nuclear deterrent and the opposition (54% in the most recent polls) to the stationing of US missiles in this country. But does all this amount to anti-Americanism?

In the Gallup Poll of March 1982, 56% expressed some confidence that if Britain's security were threatened by the USSR, America would do whatever was necessary in its defence, even if it meant risking an attack upon itself. Only 25% believe that having American troops stationed in Britain increases its vulnerability to attack, while 70% feel that they, too, either provide greater protection or have no effect.

As with other long-term trends in the public's views about defence, there appears to have been considerable stability in opinion about the military aspects of Atlantic relations for many years. Recent fluctuations have arisen out of much the same concerns which have influenced public opinion in the past, especially confidence in the wisdom of the authorities in Washington. There is, however, one important qualification to this. Left-wing supporters and the young are less favourably inclined towards the United States, NATO and defence matters in general than older people and Conservative Party supporters, although the differences are not as great as some would imagine. The most significant disparity in opinion is over the deployment of US nuclear forces and troops in Britain, with 53% of Labour Party supporters thinking they increased the risk to the country's security, as compared with only 23% of Conservatives who object to their presence here.[21]

The same stability of long-term trends is apparent in attitudes towards the West European allies. There is a tendency for people to state their willingness to give greater support to allies in more threatening and troubled circumstances, such as the aftermath of the Afghanistan crisis, but at other times a majority has stated its preference not to get involved in other people's troubles.

There is one important final point to be made about the attitude of the British public towards the Alliance. In so far as it does reflect views inconsistent with membership of NATO, then this might be part of a much broader attitude than the much-discussed phenomenon of anti-Americanism. For, in general, there does appear to be a noticeable tendency among the public to wish to opt out of international affairs, and in late 1981 some 46% thought that Britain should become neutral. For a number of years now, the polls have shown that at least 50% of the public would have preferred to see Britain more like Sweden or Switzerland than trying to be a leading world power.[22] There is no evidence of any recent upturn in favour of neutralism or, for that matter, in favour of Britain's adopting a more isolationist position in international affairs. But it is important to appreciate that such an attitude exists and that it is fairly strong. In a troubled and dangerous world, it is this tendency which might colour attitudes towards such controversial subjects as INF, rather than any new-found sympathies or sea-changes in traditional trends of opinion.

4 The Netherlands

To the outsider, Dutch politics can be a confusing series of puzzles. The political party system is certainly complicated: since World War II, over twenty parties representing religious, economic and ideological interests have competed in at least one election. The foreign policy traditions of the Netherlands are equally complex. On the one hand, there is a strong pacifist, some would say anti-militarist, tradition, a result not only of the influence of law and religion on Dutch thinking about international affairs, but also of the historical antipathy of commercial interests to the costs, and presumably influence, of a large standing army.[1]

On the other hand, the moralist/pacifist tradition is balanced by an equally strong strain of rationalism and pragmatism. As one native observer pointed out in 1982, the traditional Dutch interest in international law served not only to promote a more organized world order but also to frame the pursuit of maritime and commercial interests.[2] Similarly, the Dutch aversion to 'power politics' did not preclude a period of colonial expansion.

Furthermore, despite pacifist traditions, since 1949 the military alliance in NATO has been supported by a broad consensus. Of course, membership of NATO represents a break with another Dutch tradition, what Voorhoeve calls 'abstentionism' in foreign policy. According to Voorhoeve, 'neutralism' and 'isolationism' are inaccurate descriptions of the foreign policy of the Dutch, since neither legal neutrality nor complete withdrawal have characterized their actions. Instead, abstention from power politics has been the standard, a standard followed even during World War I.[3]

If NATO brought an end to the abstentionist tradition, this was due both to the failure of the policy in World War II and to the necessity of securing Dutch interests in the new power situation that resulted from the war. Although the Netherlands did not directly confront the Soviet Union on the dividing line of Europe, the tensions of the Cold War were sufficient to cause a triumph of pragmatic alliance politics over the traditions of pacifism and abstentionism.[4]

None the less, recent events in the Netherlands have placed the country at the centre of discussions about 'neutralism' and 'pacifism' in NATO. In fact, public questioning of NATO policy has been seen by some as a uniquely Dutch disease. Certainly activism in the Netherlands has influenced public opinion in other European countries. Increasingly, moreover, Dutch public opinion has raised questions about the durability of the post-World War II consensus on the necessity, if not the virtue, of military alliance in NATO.

The priority of defence

Despite the prominence of the Dutch peace movement, the public at large is much like that of other NATO members when it comes to the amount of attention given to security issues. In the late 1970s, about 30–40% claimed to read about defence policy, a figure approximating that of the 'informed public' in other countries.[5] In 1982, about the same number (42%) agreed that 'it is certainly possible for non-experts to understand the essentials of defence problems'. The percentage of the younger age groups who agreed with this statement is only slightly larger than that of the public in general (48%).[6]

The Dutch also resemble other countries in the low priority accorded to security issues. Defence received the *least* attention of several issues posed in a 1977 survey, and the priority of defence has remained low relative to other problems over the past few years (Table 3). Despite almost constant debate over nuclear weapons and East–West relations in general, in mid-1982 only 4% of a national survey mentioned disarmament, 'nuclear weapons out' or less defence spending as the most important tasks for the incoming government, while 80% mentioned social issues.[7]

The low priority of security issues is hardly due to a complacent or

Table 3 Important policy problems in the Netherlands: percentage responding that the problem is a 'great problem' or a 'very great problem' (excluding non-response and those with no opinion)

	1977	1977	1978	1978	1978	1978	1979	1980	1980	1980
Unemployment	94	95	95	95	93	93	91	92	95	96
Air/water pollution	86	87	89	87	89	89	89	89	88	85
Crime	94	93	93	88	90	88	93	91	91	86
Abuse of social security	86	82	86	80	82	86	86	85	87	84
Housing shortage	66	68	74	74	72	74	72	88	87	82
Nuclear power	70	76	76	69	80	69	77	79	77	77
Income distribution	63	68	63	61	62	63	63	67	69	64
Abortion	62	57	58	60	59	58	61	61	65	62
Defence	45	51	48	41	47	51	50	51	54	54
Development aid	58	54	54	51	55	54	56	54	53	48
Labour participation	44	49	46	43	38	43	41	44	34	35
N	(583)	(594)	(606)	(599)	(598)	(598)	(633)	(578)	(627)	(599)

Source: 11, Waves 15–23 (DCS).

benign view of Soviet capabilities and intentions. In a poll conducted in 1974, a minimum of 65% believed that 'a military counterbalance [is necessary] in Western Europe to offset the power of Russia and the other countries of Eastern Europe', and this view is strongly held even among the normally more dovish Labour Party (PvdA). In fact, belief in the necessity of military forces has declined only slightly since 1963: 82% of the public believed in 1982 that the Dutch armed forces were 'necessary' or a 'necessary evil'.[8]

Nevertheless, the Dutch do not believe that a Soviet attack is imminent or even that the Soviet Union will intimidate the West politically. This attitude is revealed in polls conducted since the Soviet invasion of Afghanistan; in July 1980, 53% felt that 'Russia is not a serious danger to Western Europe', and in March 1981 only about 35% were worried about a Soviet attack or political pressure on Western Europe.[9]

In summary, despite the widespread publicity accompanying the actions of the Dutch peace movement, opinion surveys reveal a national profile that is not unlike that of other countries. Interest in security issues is evident only among a minority, and the population at large finds domestic issues of far greater interest and import. Although the level of threat perceived by the population is generally low, the perceived need for a deterrent, a military counterbalance, is high. Thus, while the Dutch share the economic and social preoccupations of public opinion in all NATO countries, there does not appear to have been a drastic departure from the pragmatism of post-World War II views on defence. For the Dutch, the defence effort may be *contre coeur*, but it is necessary none the less.

Defence spending and national priorities

The Netherlands faces the prospect of severe constraints on the public budget to perhaps an even greater extent than other Western countries. Dutch governments can appeal to a general feeling among the population that the government's budget should be balanced. In 1967 and 1972, surveys showed clear majorities favouring cuts in public spending,[10] and a poll conducted in mid-1980 showed over 80% of respondents *of all political orientations* agreeing that public spending should be cut − a quite astounding degree of support.

Of course, politicians in the Netherlands as elsewhere must contend with the tendency of the public to laud fiscal responsibility while opposing cuts in specific programmes. In surveys taken over the past fifteen years, defence spending has always been listed as the least popular public priority, while housing, pollution control, social programmes and unemployment have been the most favoured. In 1980, one poll clearly marked the attitude of the Dutch to the 'defence/ welfare' question: only 21% agreed that 'it is more important to maintain our national defence than our social security'.[11]

These surveys reinforce the conclusion that public opinion is sceptical, to say the least, of increased defence spending. But they also show that the preference for civil spending is hardly new. The earliest poll mentioned above (1967) showed that 58% of respondents preferred to make cuts, if necessary, in defence rather than in other programmes. Clearly, opposition to the defence budget is not the result of a newly emerging 'anti-defence' attitude but is part of a longer-held set of priorities.

Dutch surveys on defence spending suggest that sentiments for *cutting* defence have declined, but that the change has resulted in increased support for holding defence stable rather than for increasing it. In summary, although the Dutch are slightly more sceptical of the defence budget than is public opinion in other NATO countries, the general pattern is much the same. Although the public is not overwhelmingly hostile to the defence budget when the issue is posed in isolation (about one-third favour cuts), neither is it enthusiastic about increases. Civilian programmes are the clear priority of a society that is accustomed to improvement in living standards and is concerned about continuing domestic needs, such as adequate housing and water quality. As is the case in other NATO countries, the Dutch government must deal with these priorities as it attempts to control public spending.

Nuclear weapons out?

We noted above that there are both pragmatic and pacifist elements to Dutch thinking about foreign policy. A similar duality appears to characterize thinking about nuclear weapons, a subject on which there have been more numerous surveys than in any country covered in this book.[12]

A pragmatic or 'realist' impression emerges from a poll conducted in early 1982, after several years of vocal debate over NATO's 1979 modernization decision. 60% of the public attributed the absence of war in Europe wholly or partly to the existence of nuclear weapons; 43% felt that defence without nuclear weapons was impossible; and a majority of 51% believed that in any event 'we'll have to learn to live with nuclear weapons'. Of course, these attitudes do not mean that the Dutch are positive about the nuclear element of NATO strategy. In fact, when one examines the polls further, the picture that emerges is one of antipathy tempered by a perceived obligation to fulfil NATO commitments and to await the results of negotiations for arms limitation.

The essentially negative Dutch attitude towards the weapons themselves is revealed by the level of acceptance of the slogan of the Inter-Church Council (IKV): 'Free the world of nuclear weapons and let it begin with the Netherlands.' In polls conducted in 1978 and 1981, majorities supported the slogan. Nor is this attitude new; since 1975, the polls have consistently revealed a majority opposing nuclear tasks as part of the Dutch defence effort.[13]

Yet opposition to nuclear weapons is conditioned by other considerations. For example, in 1979 one survey asked whether nuclear weapons should be removed from the Netherlands or if removal was 'not yet possible'; 50% chose the latter response. In 1979 and 1980, 49% felt that nuclear weapons were 'necessary to West European armament', and that 'one hopes that nuclear weapons will never be used . . . [but] Western Europe must nevertheless have nuclear weapons at its disposal . . . '. When asked in 1979 whether the Netherlands should disarm unilaterally or continue to negotiate for multilateral disarmament, 76% chose negotiation.[14] Also in 1979, only 13% felt that the IKV slogan could be implemented unilaterally, while 74% felt that it could be acted upon 'only after discussions and agreement with other NATO countries'.[15]

The willingness to defer unilateral actions has apparently influenced attitudes to INF deployment as well. Throughout 1981 there was growing acceptance of the deploy/negotiate options. As uncertainty declined (perhaps in response to President Reagan's actions), support for the negotiating options grew to 43%. However, *opposition* to INF also crystallized during this period, so that by late 1981 a majority opposed INF deployment unconditionally. But it is worth noting that opposition is much stronger when deployment of INF is posed *without* mention of a negotiating option. As many as 56% opposed deployment, despite the fact that an ominous cue on Soviet deployments was included in the question; 47% opposed deployment when negotiating options were mentioned.

Perhaps the most interesting aspect of these surveys is their resemblance to the West German polls. Like West Germans, the Dutch are generally negative about nuclear weapons, but they are not totally 'rejectionist' when the weapons are described in the context of NATO obligations or as part of a bilateral negotiation. Like West Germans, the Dutch also reject the *use* of nuclear weapons, despite the grudging acceptance of deterrence arguments; precisely 50% are unwilling to consider using them under any circumstances.

Dutch surveys thus reinforce the dilemma evident in the attitudes of other countries. While considerable numbers, even majorities, appear resigned to the need for nuclear weapons as deterrents, the use of the weapons, often justified by policy-makers to reinforce deterrence, is rejected by the same majorities. This certainly explains the widespread opposition in the Netherlands to the neutron bomb, and perhaps it also illuminates opposition to the INF decision, since the latter has often been discussed as a (conscious or unconscious) change in the direction of 'decoupling', and thus isolating, the European theatre.

NATO and the United States

The Dutch public has strongly supported NATO and American participation in the Alliance. In fact, given the visibility and intensity of recent Atlantic debates, the constancy of support for NATO is surprising. In 1977, the percentage of poll respondents who thought NATO 'necessary for peace in Europe' was slightly higher than in 1971 (75% versus 71%).[16] In 1981, over 60% of the Dutch felt that NATO was 'still essential' to their security, and similar numbers (61%) agreed in 1982 that 'only as a member of NATO can the Netherlands effectively defend itself'.[17] Given these figures, it is hardly surprising that sentiment to withdraw from NATO has never been strong. An average of about 75% prefer to remain in NATO, and the percentage favouring withdrawal has never exceeded 16%. Perhaps most striking, in 1982 only 27% advocated leaving NATO even if the Alliance 'holds on to nuclear weapons'.[18]

Opinions of the United States are more mixed, depending on whether the question raises the more general issue of the American 'image' or relates to the pragmatic issue of the need for an American security guarantee. On the latter, there is a firm majority. In fact, although the questions were not identical, surveys in 1977 and 1982 suggest that those perceiving a need for American security participation in NATO have actually risen slightly, to 62%.

Broader evaluations of American policy are far less favourable. For example, surveys by the American government document a sharp decline in the overall image of the United States, from 65% favourable in 1978 to 46% in 1981.[19] During 1981, moreover, there was an increase in the percentage of the Dutch who answered 'not very much' or 'none at all' to the question of confidence in the ability of the United States to deal responsibly with world problems.

In general, then, Dutch views on NATO and the United States parallel those in other countries: NATO is seen as essential, despite critical attitudes towards the United States. Perhaps this should not surprise us, since public opinion confirms influential scholarly analyses of the Atlantic security relationship. As several authors have argued, NATO has persisted despite periodic internal quarrels precisely because alternative security arrangements are unfeasible, unpopular, or both.[20]

Summary and conclusions

Much has been made of the term 'Hollanditis'. Indeed, the term itself suggests that there is something about Dutch opinion and politics that is unique. None the less, it is easier to decide what Hollanditis is *not* than to ascribe a special place to public opinion in the Netherlands. Despite a pacifist tradition, for example, there is still evidence that the Dutch perceive a need for a deterrent to Soviet power. Furthermore, neither the abstentionist tradition nor the recent interest in 'neutralism' has captured anything like a majority in the Netherlands: the population remains solidly in favour of NATO membership.

To be sure, there is little support for *increasing* military strength through additional defence spending, but this attitude is hardly peculiar to the Netherlands. Nor are Dutch attitudes towards nuclear weapons particularly distinctive, with a generally negative sentiment suppressed only by the need for Alliance coordination or the prospect of arms control. On the INF issue, Dutch opinion seems to have crystallized at a point of evenly divided opinion, with figures quite close to recent polls in other countries.

If the Netherlands has a special feature, it is in the impact of opinion, rather than in the levels of support and denial. Especially on the INF issue, the visibility and intensity of opposition has prevented the Dutch government from final adoption of the NATO position, whereas other NATO governments have remained committed despite heavy domestic pressure. As we have seen, the hesitancy of the Dutch government occurs despite the fact that a potential majority, however slim, is receptive to arguments concerning Soviet deployments and Alliance coordination.

The caution of Dutch governments probably results from two considerations. First, there is a fear that acceptance of the 1979 decision, should it result in actual deployment, could lead to further protest and perhaps to civil disobedience and violence. Second, the widespread belief that governments must embark on a course of severe budgetary retrenchment suggests that substantial amounts of political capital must be reserved for the considerable debate that will surely follow.

The nuclear and budgetary issues highlight the precariousness of parliamentary coalitions. In the first place, political positions do not always match the general thrust of party policy. The existence of a 'progressive minority' in the Christian Democratic Appeal ensures that some opposition to INF and social spending cuts will come from *within* the leading party of the governing coalition. In the second, as Domke has argued, the decline of traditional attachments to confessional parties has been accompanied by an increase in issue-based, 'populist' swings from election to election.[21] Since coalition majorities are thin to begin with, even minor swings could change election outcomes.

Of course, the fragility of parliamentary majorities is probably not a result of security issues. One might argue that the condition of the Dutch, indeed all European, party systems has evolved both from long-term social changes and from short-term economic factors. In this sense, security policy in the Netherlands, as elsewhere, must be seen as part of a more general problem of consensus in contemporary democratic societies. But even this realization should not obscure the fact that, in general outline, the consensus surrounding security policy is intact, however intense the recent scrutiny of specific choices.

5 Norway and Denmark

Of the five countries in the Nordic region, Norway, Denmark and
Iceland have sought to augment their security by membership of
NATO; Sweden and Finland have preferred to remain neutral and have
not aligned themselves formally with either the Western or the Eastern
bloc. However, Nordic security has depended upon Sweden and
Finland maintaining a significant defence effort and doing their utmost
to safeguard their neutrality. Because of their national defence postures
it has been far easier than it might otherwise have been for NATO
to concur with Denmark and Norway in banning all nuclear weapons
from their territory in peacetime and not allowing any permanent
foreign (NATO) bases on their soil.

In this chapter we shall be considering the state of public opinion
in relation to defence in two of the Nordic members of the Atlantic
Alliance, Norway and Denmark. In these countries, disarmament is
reported to be a major political issue, and the delicacy of their relationship with their neutral Nordic neighbours has meant that until recently
NATO as a whole was less preoccupied with that area than with the
Central Front. Indeed, until the last decade or so, the naval forces
of the United States and Britain constituted the principal deterrent
to any Soviet attack on Denmark and Norway. This was largely because, as elsewhere in Europe, the Warsaw Pact's advantage lay in its
preponderance of conventional ground forces. In every other respect,
the advantage lay with the Alliance.

Nowadays things are different. Not only are the ground forces
available to the Warsaw Pact vastly superior to those of the West, but
there is also a naval and air balance in the area. The United States has

lost its virtual automatic right of access to northern Soviet targets, and the British Navy has abandoned its large-deck aircraft carriers. The Soviet Northern Fleet, by contrast, is constantly increasing the size and versatility of the vessels available to protect its territory as well as mount a formidable offensive. In the air, the Soviet Backfire aircraft constitutes a powerful threat to US carrier forces in the Atlantic, as well as to the convoys that would reinforce US forces in Europe in time of war, and to existing key NATO installations in the North Atlantic area.

It was because of these developments that, from the mid-1970s onwards, increasing attention had to be paid to the growing imbalance between the NATO and Warsaw Pact capabilities in the Nordic area. This meant focusing attention on Norway and Denmark, with the aim of alleviating the burden on the United States and the other Alliance partners and thereby rectifying the balance as far as possible. Most has been achieved, in this respect, in relation to the defence of northern Norway. This region, comprising the provinces of Finnmark and Troms, had come to be regarded as being particularly vulnerable to Soviet attack because of the strategic advantage that control of the area would give the USSR in time of war. Its loss would deprive NATO of early-warning information of Soviet movements in the Kola; and it would give the Soviet Union additional protection for those of its forces based in the region.

The solution to NATO's dilemma, therefore, had come to be seen in terms of a combination of a so-called pre-stocking of equipment in Norway and the rapid deployment by air of American ground forces to buttress Norway's thin defences in the area in time of crisis. Sensitive to the Soviet Union's susceptibilities about the threat to its security in the far north, Norway has traditionally limited its active forces there to a small brigade. These were to be reinforced by reserves, which in turn were to be supplemented by NATO naval forces in time of crisis. But the deterrent value of the latter had been undermined by the improvement in Soviet capabilities.

Negotiations between the United States and Norway about the pre-stocking of equipment in the northern area began in the late 1970s and were based upon the principle that the locating of equipment rather than personnel would not conflict with Norway's traditional policy of not permitting foreign bases on its soil. They were completed successfully in January 1981, with the announcement of a Pre-stocking Agreement which has been regarded as a major step towards restoring the credibility of NATO's northernmost defences. In particular, it involved a combination of upgrading Norwegian forces in the region and more tangible evidence of a US commitment to assist in Norway's defence. It is against this background that expressions of public opinion about defence in Norway need to be evaluated.[1]

In the case of Denmark, the situation is less satisfactory from NATO's point of view. In the face of clear signs of a significant build-up of Warsaw Pact forces in the southern part of the Northern Front, and what appear to be determined efforts to establish Soviet dominance in the Baltic, the Danes have been among the most reluctant of all members of the Alliance to increase their defence spending. Moreover, they have seemed to be moving towards reducing their defence spending at a time when the NATO governments generally had decided to embark upon a real growth of at least 3%. This attitude has caused friction between Denmark and the United States, where it was feared that Denmark was heading for the same kind of neutrality that proximity to the Soviet Union has imposed upon Finland. Since the Reagan administration came to power in the United States, relations with Denmark have, if anything, deteriorated further. Danish defence spending remains well below the 3% annual increase agreed by Alliance members in 1977. The Danes have shown no enthusiasm whatsoever for the deployment of theatre nuclear weapons in Europe and have even expressed their sympathy for Soviet INF proposals. In addition, although Denmark is heavily dependent on oil imports from the Arabian Gulf, there has been little support among the Danes for any Western initiatives outside the NATO area.[2]

Finally, the United States has been very reluctant to enter into the kind of pre-stocking arrangement that it negotiated so successfully with the Norwegians for fear that the supply of US equipment to Denmark would provide the Danes with further opportunities to reduce, rather than increase, their defence spending. It is in this context that popular attitudes in Denmark need to be seen.

Perceptions of the threat

Norway's membership of the Alliance is based upon the assumption that the country is unable to defend itself against foreign aggression and that it can deter attack only with external assistance prepared for in advance. Membership of the Alliance, involving such arrangements as the Pre-stocking Agreement with the United States and regular Allied manoeuvres on its territory, has been seen as reinforcing in the mind of any potential aggressor the idea that any attack on Norway would inevitably trigger off a wider conflict.

Awareness of Norway's strategic vulnerability in the north, backed up by persistent memories of its experience prior to the German attack in 1940, probably accounts for the remarkable stability, as well as high level, of public support for maintaining the country's military defence establishment. Since 1973, the figure for those in favour of maintaining Norway's defence effort has never fallen below 75% of the population, while since 1979 it has never been less than 80% (see Table 4). Moreover, during the past decade, public concern about the international situation has been high, with never less than two-thirds of respondents to opinion polls stating their belief that international relations were either very or rather tense. From 1979 onwards, people's perception of international tensions rose to an even higher level. In 1981, for example, 53% believed that international relations were very tense and a further 37% thought they were rather tense.[3] There can be little doubt, therefore, that in Norway, as throughout the Alliance countries (with the possible exception of France), public concern about the state of the world is high, and that this underlies the general support for the nation's defence effort. At the same time, it causes disquiet about particular aspects of defence policy which are regarded as adding to rather than preventing risks to national security.

To turn now to Danish perceptions of the 'threat', it is important to note that at least during the past century there has existed a strand of political opinion which has insisted that the country is so vulnerable that it cannot be defended. In the 1973 elections, Mogens Glistrup, the leader of the populist Progress Party, which became the second largest party in the Danish parliament, proposed that Danish defence

Table 4 Attitudes towards military defence in Norway, 1973–82 (%)
Q: 'Do you consider that Norway should maintain a military defence establishment in the present situation?'

	1973	1974	1975	1976	1977	1978	1979	1980	1981	1982
Yes	75	79	75	79	79	79	84	86	80	86
No	10	7	6	5	7	6	6	4	6	6
Uncertain	8	9	11	9	8	10	7	5	6	3
Don't know	7	5	8	8	6	5	4	6	8	5
Total	100	100	100	100	100	100	100	100	100	100
N	1635	1593	1659	1599	1675	1675	1709	1437	1376	1404

Source: Johan Jørgen Holst, 'Norwegian Security Policy', *Cooperation and Conflict*, vol. 17, no. 4 (1982), p. 216.

policy should consist of closing down the armed services and replacing them by an automatic telephone answering device which, if Denmark were to be attacked, would answer 'We surrender' in Russian. Glistrup was reflecting a pacifist strand in Danish opinion which goes back to the nineteenth century, when the slogan was 'What is the Use?' and which helps to explain why Denmark has appeared to be one of the weaker links in the Alliance.

Nevertheless, Denmark's defence policy rests upon its relationship with the West. This takes the form of an Alliance guarantee to reinforce its forces if the country is attacked; it remains firmly attached to the principle of deterrence, and, like Norway, to maintaining its national sovereignty in peacetime, which has meant refusing to allow nuclear weapons or foreign bases on its territory. Moreover, despite their determination to maintain a reputation for promoting détente and disarmament, the Danes do not play down the fact that they regard Soviet policy as the main reason for international tension, and this view appears to be supported by the bulk of public opinion. Thus, for example, in a poll conducted in August 1980 53% believed that the Soviet Union presented a greater threat to the security of Western Europe than the United States. Only 5% mentioned the latter, although 20% believed that in the long run both superpowers threatened Europe's security.[4] Right across the Alliance the majority view is that the Warsaw Pact has far stronger conventional forces than NATO, and the Danes are no exception to this. They also believe that the Warsaw Pact is stronger when nuclear weapons are taken into account.

Danish public opinion is particularly pessimistic about the possibility that Denmark's defence forces would be able to hold their ground in the event of an attack while waiting for help from NATO to arrive. By a ratio of three to one, people believe that temporary Danish defence is impossible.[5] On the other hand, twice as many people take the view that the only possibility for peaceful coexistence between East and West lies in a mutual military threat as those who believe in the possibility of agreement between the blocs. Finally, Danish public opinion coincides completely with the view of the overwhelming majority across the Alliance in its pessimism about the future. In November 1980, for example, 62% believed that 1981 would be a more troubled year than 1980, and only 3% believed it would be a year of peace.[6]

Defence expenditure

In Norway, regardless of which party has been in power, defence expenditure has remained steady – at around 3% of GNP – over the past decade (see Table 5). In fact, Norway has ranked fourth in NATO in terms of defence expenditure per capita, following only behind the three nuclear powers, the USA, France and Britain. Moreover, in real terms, the defence budget grew by 2.8%, 1.5%, and 2.8% in 1979, 1980 and 1981 respectively.[7]

Table 5   Norwegian defence expenditures as a percentage of GNP

1977	1978	1979	1980	1981	1982	1983
3.3%	3.2%	3.1%	2.8%	2.9%	2.9%	3.0%

Source: St. prp. nr.1 (1982/3), Forsvarsdepartementet, in Holst, 'Norwegian Security Policy', loc. cit., p. 231.

Nevertheless, as in other NATO countries, public opinion assigns to defence a very low priority when compared with other national purposes. A typical example is a poll taken in 1967, a year of high international tension following a major Middle East war. Only 2.5% of those asked would have assigned high priority to defence, compared with 51% who mentioned housing, 41% assistance to the handicapped, 21% health and 18% welfare.[8]

In Denmark, by contrast, defence expenditure has been a major issue. The economy has continued to suffer from relative stagnation, and the government has faced internal pressures for avoiding real increases in defence spending. Paradoxically, however, the level of defence expenditure has been a matter of controversy less for the general public than in Danish political circles. In 1980, a Gallup Poll put the question to its respondents in considerable detail. It stated that Denmark had failed to fulfil its obligations to the Alliance and that the country was being strongly urged to increase defence expenditure. The choices facing it, therefore, were whether in real terms to increase spending, to maintain spending at the same level or to cut expenditure. In reply, 61% wanted defence spending either to be kept at the present level or to be increased, only 26% wanted it reduced and the remainder had no opinion either way.[9] Later in the same year, however, in reply to a question asking whether more money should be made available if Denmark was unable to meet NATO planning targets or whether the defence effort should be downgraded to match the resources currently available, 44% were against increasing spending, only 30% favoured spending more and the remainder had no opinion. Moreover, in the same poll, of those expressing any opinion (about two-thirds of respondents), 53% would have earmarked money for overseas development aid rather than defence, and the remaining 47% favoured defence.[11]

In sum, then, Danish public opinion is very much in line with opinion throughout the Alliance. When asked about defence spending in isolation, two-thirds of the population are broadly in favour of such allocations as governments are prepared to make, but support falls away dramatically in response to so-called trade-off questions. Public priorities, too, follow the trend in other NATO countries, although in the Danish case this is buttressed by the view that Denmark's strategic importance virtually guarantees that the allies will come to its assistance in time of need.

Nuclear weapons

Norway and Denmark have consistently pursued a policy of refusing to store and deploy nuclear weapons on their territory in peacetime, nor are their forces trained in their use. The caveat 'in peacetime' is not without significance, especially in the Danish case. It is a new formulation, announced by the Danish foreign minister in 1980, and replaces an earlier one, which was 'during the present conditions'. It is believed that the new formula is more precise and direct, since it involves the possibility of a policy change in times of crisis.

Between the early 1960s and 1979, nuclear weapons did not provoke any discussion or controversy in Norway. In November 1964, 78% of respondents to a poll considered it advantageous not to have nuclear weapons in Norway, compared with 56% who were of this opinion in 1961. In a survey published in January 1980, 79% stated that Norway should continue to refuse the deployment or stockpiling of nuclear weapons on its soil; only 10% favoured any change in this policy.[12] Indeed, there is no significant controversy over the issue; rather, the debate is about NATO adopting a possible 'no first use' policy. Norway's participation in NATO's Nuclear Planning Group has meant that it has been fully involved in the INF controversy, and it was prominent in formulating the dual-track decision in December 1979. From the start, it took the view that final policy had to be decided in the light of the concrete results of the negotiations with the Russians, and that there should be no automatic deployment of the new intermediate-range nuclear weapons. Moreover, the Norwegians insisted that, in view of their policy of not basing nuclear weapons on their territory, Norway should not be one of the deploying countries.

The government of the day was able to secure approval for the NATO decision by only one vote in the country's parliament. Public opinion was opposed to it, and in a poll taken in January 1980 only 37% favoured the dual-track proposal, while 44% were against. One consequence of the episode, however, was increased public interest in the idea of a nuclear-free zone in the Nordic area. The Norwegian Labour Party, at its April 1981 conference, proposed that Norway should work towards the establishment of such a zone as part of the effort to reduce nuclear weapons within a broader European framework. But support for the unilateral creation of such a zone on the part of the Nordic countries is low. In a poll conducted in 1981, 59% considered that as a condition of establishing such a zone the northern area of the Soviet Union must be included. Moreover, in polls in 1981 and in 1982 69% and 65%, respectively, were reported as believing that the Nordic states should deal with the matter of a nuclear-free zone in the context of NATO's negotiations with the Warsaw Pact. It is significant that in another poll only 26% of the Norwegian population believed that the Soviet Union would respect its commitment to such a zone, while 66% believed that it would not.[13]

In contrast to the Labour Party, the Conservatives in Norway are much more sceptical about the idea of a nuclear-free zone, although their allies in the Centre and Christian People's Parties have adopted a platform almost identical with that of Labour. There are, however, differences over NATO's and Scandinavian attitudes towards nuclear policy which could threaten the consensus about defence which has existed in Norway for many years. In this respect, Norway is again very similar to the other members of the Alliance and conforms to the general pattern which has emerged throughout this study.

Danish public opinion on nuclear weapons is close to that of Norway. Any differences between the two countries are too small to be significant. The Danes are highly sceptical of American claims that the Alliance is now lagging far behind the Soviet Union in respect of its nuclear capability. However, there remains the widespread belief that the concept of Mutual Assured Destruction provides the best guarantee for world peace at this time and will continue to do so pending the successful outcome of arms reduction talks between the superpowers. In Denmark, despite its reputation, support for unilateral nuclear disarmament by members of the Alliance, regardless of what the Warsaw Pact countries might do, seems to be no higher than anywhere else in the NATO countries.

Alliance relationships

In comparison with the superpowers and the middle-ranking powers of Europe, both Norway and Denmark are very small and vulnerable states. They depend for their defence on their membership of the Atlantic Alliance. In the case of Norway, the lesson learned in 1940 was that arrangements have to be made in peacetime for any assistance that may be needed in time of war. In comparison with other Alliance members, Norway's contribution to NATO has remained at a fairly high level. In Denmark's case, it is more a question of the Alliance doing for Denmark what the Danes are unwilling as well as unable to do for themselves.

In both countries, leaving aside particular issues, public support for membership of the Alliance is both stable and high. In Norway's case, over the period from 1973 to 1981, never less than two out of every three Norwegians have believed that membership of NATO has contributed towards the country's security (see Table 6). In another poll in September 1981, in response to a more direct question, 79% of respondents declared themselves in favour of NATO membership, with only 16% against. Election studies carried out between 1965 and 1977 showed a steady increase in the proportion of those who supported Norway's continued membership of NATO (see Table 7).

Table 6 Norwegian attitudes to NATO membership, 1973–81 (%)

Q: 'Do you think that Norway's membership in the Western defence alliance (NATO) contributes towards securing the country against attacks from a foreign power, or are you of the opinion that our membership of NATO increases the danger of attack, or do you think that our NATO membership is of no consequence in this respect?'

	1973 Nov	1974 Nov	1975 Nov	1976 Nov	1977 Nov	1978 Nov	1979 Nov	1980 Jan	1980 Nov	1981 Nov
Contributes toward securing the country	61	61	62	65	62	64	62	66	60	64
Increases the danger of attack	7	5	6	6	8	6	10	7	14	10
Makes no difference	14	17	14	11	12	10	10	11	10	9
Don't know	18	17	19	18	19	20	18	16	15	17
Total	100	100	101	100	101	100	100	100	100	100
N	2102	1574	1649	1515	1607	1614	1520	1519	1499	1348

Source: Kontakt Bulletin, published by Folk og Forsvar, nos. 1/2, 1982, pp. 3–9, in Holst, 'Norwegian Security Policy', loc.cit., p. 215.

Table 7   Norwegian attitudes to NATO membership, 1965-77 (%)

Q: 'Many people consider that we should hold on to the NATO alliance, while others think that our membership should be discontinued. What is your opinion?

	1965	1969	1973	1977
Of those with an opinion:				
Continue membership	75	79	86	89
Discontinue membership	25	21	14	11
N	1623	1595	1225	1730

Source: As Table 6. Don't knows excluded.

There is therefore no question that although there may be criticism of certain policies of the Alliance, the overwhelming majority of Norwegians are in favour of their government pursuing a defence policy in the context of NATO, and there is little if any support for any Nordic or neutralist alternative.

In Denmark, in the 1980s, there has been a shift towards what more people outside than inside the country have called Denmarkization. In so far as this has any meaning at all, it suggests that while Denmark has security problems which it shares with the other members of the Alliance, it also has national security goals consisting of aspirations towards a policy of non-confrontation and non-provocation. Denmark has no natural resources, and therefore feels obliged to pursue a more outward policy towards the primary producer countries of the Third World than do other Alliance members. In addition, as noted, there is a tradition of pacifism which, by extension, involves a Western-oriented Denmark adopting a neutral stance in international relations.

None the less, in contrast to all this, Danish public opinion has consistently supported membership of NATO. In the late 1970s and early 1980s, the polls showed regularly that over twice as many people were in favour of membership of the Alliance as those who were against it. The only favoured alternative is not isolation or any arrangement with the Eastern bloc, but membership of some neutral Scandinavian alliance. This is very much a hypothetical possibility, arising out of fears about NATO's nuclear policies and a concern, widespread elsewhere in the Alliance, that the superpowers might between them involve their allies in wars in which Denmark has no interest. But even in a poll which showed that 41% would prefer Denmark to join forces with the other Scandinavian countries to form a neutral bloc, 44% preferred Denmark to cooperate with NATO as regards its security policy, and no respondents envisaged any arrangement with the Warsaw Pact.[14]

In conclusion, although obvious differences exist, neither Norway nor Denmark has any practical alternatives to pursuing their defence policies in the context of the Alliance, and this view is held at least as strongly among their general publics as among those of any other NATO country. The Scandinavian members of NATO exemplify the diversity, and at the same time the underlying community of interests, which characterize the Atlantic Alliance. Although regional and national factors cause them to diverge from certain fundamental aspects of the Alliance, particularly as regards nuclear weapons and basing policies, there also exists a degree of interdependence which in most important respects supersedes the differences. Sudden fluctuations in public opinion seem unlikely to undermine this.

6 France

Public opinion in France, like that in the other countries considered, is divided between those who take a special interest in defence and the vast majority, for whom it is of little everyday concern. The only difference, and it is an interesting and important one, is that there has been a major growth in interest over the past decade among the country's elites. Under the presidencies of de Gaulle and Pompidou, national security policy was left almost exclusively in the domain of the president. Whatever their views, even those closest to the centre of power (in the government and parliament, officials, academics and even the media) were content to go along with whatever the Elysée determined.

This was not because de Gaulle changed the substance of French foreign policy in the direction desired by those who sought his return to power in 1958. Both his settlement of the Algerian crisis and his acceptance of the European Economic Community were extremely controversial and ran counter to orthodox opinion. Moreover, it was not de Gaulle's decision for France to build its own atomic weapon; that had already been decided under the previous regime of the Fourth Republic.

The reason was that for de Gaulle, in contrast to his predecessors, foreign policy was all. Domestic, economic and social policies were merely the means to enable France to pursue its goal of recovering its rightful place in the world.[1] The general public supported de Gaulle's foreign and defence policies because they embodied a number of national aspirations. Above all, there was the excision of the 'shame of 1940', when France became the only major world power to surrender during World War II. Along with this was the determination that the country would never again be betrayed; its territory would remain, as far as possible, unviolated by foreign invaders. In addition, there was de Gaulle's determination that France needed to be independent in a dangerous world of military alliances: a part of the West, but as far as possible in a position to influence the course of world affairs and in particular the policies of the senior partner, the United States. All this was widely shared by the overwhelming majority of Frenchmen. It is still the major strand underlying popular sentiment, long after de Gaulle's departure from the political stage.

The possession of an independent nuclear deterrent and the maintenance of sizeable conventional forces, in alliance with NATO but independently controlled, has been the cornerstone of French defence policy throughout most of the Fifth Republic. Indeed there has been no perceptible change since the Socialists came to power in 1981 — this in spite of the fact that it was they who were initially responsible for such debate as began to evolve among the so-called 'attentive publics' after Giscard d'Estaing became president in 1974. Faced with the prospect of power, the Socialists, under the leadership of the man who was to become defence minister, Charles Hernu, had to engage in internal debates over defence which they had previously avoided for fear of disruptive consequences. (There is still a strong pacifist element within the French Socialist Party.) The Communist Party has also had to deal with this question, and has supported both the retention of France's independent nuclear deterrent and its continuing membership of NATO. On the right, among the opposition parties, there is controversy between those Gaullists who wish to remain faithful to the policies of the General and some supporters of Giscard d'Estaing who favour a return to NATO's joint military command.[2]

Unlike Britain and West Germany, however, there still exists a broad consensus about defence among the 'attentive publics' which seems to extend right across the political spectrum. Such differences as do exist are more of emphasis than substance. It is possibly because of the absence of serious controversy in political circles that the one phenomenon which has provoked so much dissension among the other European members of the Alliance is absent in France: there is no significant movement for unilateral nuclear disarmament. This is not to say that there is less concern in France about the dangers of nuclear war than elsewhere; it is rather that, in the French case, the broad public acceptance of current defence policy which, we are suggesting, actually prevails throughout the Alliance has not been obscured by the existence of highly vocal protest movements.

Experience elsewhere, for example in the United Kingdom and Germany, shows that public opinion is influenced primarily by debates in political circles as they are reported in the media. In France, the lack of debate in political circles until relatively recently may mean that it is too soon for there to have been any significant impact on public opinion. The intensity of argument in periodical, daily and weekly journals of all political persuasions, and the impact of the protest movements elsewhere in Europe, could produce some change in the future. But until now the Alliance's most troublesome partner has possessed the most quiescent and supportive public opinion.

Perceptions of the threat

In all the countries we have looked at in this study the majority of people have as their main preoccupations threats to their jobs, standard of living and social security rather than concern for international peace and security. France is no exception. In one poll, published in April 1982, it was shown that throughout the previous year never more than 9% of those asked were concerned personally with the prospects for international peace.[3] This finding not only follows the pattern of other countries in Western Europe, but represents a consistent attitude over many years. Moreover, in the same poll, people thought that the country as a whole was too preoccupied with the international situation.

So far as the prospects for peace are concerned, there has been a tendency for the French to be more optimistic than the British or Germans. Between 1969 and 1979, they were on average three times as optimistic as the British about the future; only at the time of the Soviet invasion of Afghanistan did French opinion fall into line with opinion in Britain and West Germany.[4]

As for the Soviet Union, in a poll published in February 1982, 63% believed that it presented the greatest threat to world peace, while only 10% expressed a similar view about the United States and China. 76% believed that France was bound to be directly involved in any war in Europe.[5] It seems, further, that the French have a less favourable view of the Soviet Union nowadays than in the past. In November 1968, for example, only 39% believed that the Soviet Union represented a military threat to Europe; in December 1972, following the signing of the Berlin Agreement between the four great powers, only 40% believed that the Russians could be trusted, while 29% doubted the sincerity of the Soviet Union.[6] It is therefore not without irony that at a time when the Socialists are in power, and Communists serve in the government, fear of the Soviet Union should be so much greater than when they were in opposition. In a poll published in January 1983, 49% (1% more than in Britain, 4% more than in West Germany and 18% more than in the Netherlands) believed that the Soviet Union was more likely to initiate a nuclear attack in Europe than would be the United States.[7]

Despite general agreement in France over the need to defend the country, and the belief that every effort should be made to preserve its national identity, the fear of nuclear war is strong. In a poll published in October 1982, 42% put the threat of such a war among the problems which concerned them most, compared with significantly lower percentages in Germany, Britain, the Netherlands and the United States.[8]

Defence expenditure

French attitudes towards defence expenditure and the allocation of national resources for military purposes have been remarkably similar to those in the United Kingdom, and in both countries there has been considerable consistency. From 1973 until the end of 1982 approximately 65% of people questioned in polls have believed that their countries' defence spending has been either about right or too little. In one poll of October 1982, only 7% believed that Europe's financial contribution towards the defence of the West was too great; 36% thought that it was too little.[9]

The nuclear issue

Although the general public's dread of a repeat of the 'débâcle of 1940' is as great as ever, there is, as already noted, a strong fear of nuclear war. On the one hand, the polls show that the majority oppose nuclear weapons; on the other, public opinion, in so far as it believes disarmament to be possible for France, is nevertheless opposed to unilateral disarmament. In a recent poll, 40% of those asked believed that France's nuclear arsenal was either a waste of money or in itself a threat to peace. 52%, however, believed that it was either unremarkable or a necessary condition for the glory and development of France. 44% believe that general disarmament would never be possible, while 35% supported multilateral disarmament. Only 14% were prepared to begin disarming regardless of what other countries did.[10]

The fear of nuclear weapons emerges clearly in response to questions about the use of France's nuclear deterrent to defend its national territory. In May 1980, 58% of respondents to one poll opposed using the threat of France's nuclear capability if the country was on the point of being invaded, while only 28% were in favour; 72% rejected the prospect of the actual use of nuclear weapons 'as a matter of principle'.[11] In reponse to a similar question in November 1982, only 18% were in favour of using the *force de frappe* to defend French territory.[12] In February 1982, a poll asked whether its respondents would be in favour of deploying American Pershing missiles in France. Only 29% responded in the affirmative; 56% were opposed.[13] In another poll in October 1982, in response to a question on how France ought to reply to a Soviet invasion of its territory, only 10% favoured the use of nuclear weapons and, in response to a question on how France should react to a Soviet invasion of Germany, only 3% supported the use of nuclear weapons.[14]

The fear of nuclear weapons is not to be confused with pacifist tendencies. In May 1980, 52% of respondents thought that France should reject any Soviet offer of peace if the price involved accepting a militarily neutral Europe and severing the alliance with the United States. In response to a question about what people thought was worth fighting for, 79% mentioned 'freedom' and 72% 'defence of the national territory'.[15] This was confirmed in a further poll, in March

1982, when 57% stated unequivocally that however horrible a war would be it would be better to resist than to accept Soviet domination. This compared with 75% in Britain and 74% in Germany who would fight to defend their national territory rather than accept Soviet rule. However, the crucial difference in this poll was not in the percentages. Roughly the same percentage in all the countries in which the question was put, i.e. approximately 12-13%, said that they would accept Soviet rule rather than face the horror of a nuclear war. The difference lay in the numbers who were unable to express an opinion either way. In the French poll 30% replied that they did not know, compared with 13% in Britain and 7% in West Germany.[16] This result is important because it illustrates the confusion which has existed among the general public in France over defence issues throughout the life of the Fifth Republic. This confusion is exemplified also in the public's attitude towards the United States and Alliance relations.

Alliance relations

In 1966 the Atlantic Alliance was profoundly shaken by one of General de Gaulle's grand gestures. In a series of Notes to the governments of the other fourteen NATO countries, the French government announced its intention to withdraw from NATO's integrated military command. This involved the withdrawal of French military personnel from NATO's integrated headquarters and international commands and a request for the withdrawal from French territory of NATO's international headquarters, allied units and all bases independent of the control of the French authorities. The ostensible reason for de Gaulle's action was that the presence of allied military forces on French soil was an affront to France's sovereignty. But just as important was a further concern, expressed in parliamentary debates by Prime Minister Pompidou and Foreign Minister Couve de Murville, that the United States might involve its NATO allies in a nuclear war in Asia. France's independence meant having the freedom to choose its own direction in world affairs, rather than having to bow to the wishes of the senior partner in the integrated military command. Basically, de Gaulle did not trust the Americans and was determined to pursue a policy which would make France independent of the United States.[17]

Against this background, the attitude of the French public towards the Alliance comes as something of a surprise. Paradoxically, the opinion polls show that the French people have more confidence in the ability of the United States to deal wisely with world affairs than do peoples in other Alliance countries. In a Gallup Poll published in March 1982, 40% of French people were reported as having considerable or great confidence in the United States, compared with only 35% in Great Britain. 54% had either a favourable or a very favourable opinion of the United States, compared with 45% in Britain. In answer to a further question about the deployment of American missiles in Europe, only 24% believed that these missiles would increase the risks to peace, compared with 42% in Britain; 31% believed that they would give Europe greater protection, while only 29% thought this in the British case. On the question of the presence of American troops in Europe, 66% believed that their number should be maintained or even increased, only 10% wanted their number reduced, and only 11% wanted them removed altogether.[18] In another poll, published in February 1982, 80% of those asked believed that the Americans would come to the aid of Europe in an emergency. Again this contrasts with a figure of only 56% expressing some degree of confidence that America would come to Britain's aid in a poll conducted in the United Kingdom at approximately the same time.[19]

By October 1982, however, another poll produced a rather different picture. The differences can be explained in terms of the already stated concern of the French public when it comes to questions of nuclear war and atomic weapons as opposed to defence in general. In reply to a question regarding the proper American response to a Soviet attack on Western Europe, 32% stated that the Americans should react with nuclear weapons; 48%, however, thought that the Americans should negotiate for a peaceful settlement with the Soviet Union and not intervene with military force. In the same poll, the largest single percentage, 31%, expressed the belief that the best way of ensuring France's defence was through membership of a military alliance including the West European countries and the United States. Some 19% were in favour of membership of a West European alliance independent of the United States, and 18% advocated relying on France's independent capability and strengthening its own nuclear deterrent.

Only 16% held the view that France should abandon all armaments and adopt an absolutely neutral position in world affairs.[20]

Although there is great concern among the French about nuclear weapons and their possible use in any future war, all the poll evidence indicates that they are considerably more optimistic than the British about the prospects for international peace and their own security in a dangerous world. About one-third of those asked in any opinion poll have expressed the fear that there would be a third world war within the next ten to twelve years, whereas two-thirds have been optimistic about the future. In February 1982, 61% believed that their children would live in a free and independent France,[21] and the percentage of those who believe that the danger of war has increased during the last two or three years is lower in France than in most other countries in the Western Alliance, including Japan.

In conclusion, French public opinion, as reflected in the opinion polls, reveals the same stability as is to be found in the other Alliance countries and a concern for the same issue which preoccupies opinion elsewhere, namely nuclear weapons. On the other hand, the polls also reflect the absence of any significant protest movement such as exists in the non-nuclear countries of the Alliance and in the United Kingdom. In France, the shadow of 1940 still seems to influence opinion across all classes, political parties and age groups. Differences exist, but they manifest themselves mainly in response to the questions of pollsters and not in any organized form. Although it has left NATO's integrated military command, politically France remains firmly in the Western camp, and the majority of French people support the involvement in the Western Alliance, and indeed look to the Alliance for their security in the event of any future war.

7 West Germany

Much of the current concern about a 'crisis' in the Atlantic Alliance can be traced to worries about developments in the Federal Republic of Germany. Anti-nuclear demonstrations, the growth of a neutralist force (the Green Party) and the persistence of economic. recession have combined to raise questions about the ability of the Federal Republic to maintain its role as a crucial contributor to Atlantic defence. To many, even the accession of a conservative government in late 1982 brought little solace, for it freed friendly critics of the Schmidt regime from whatever responsibility they had felt for the continuation of the former coalition.

There is irony in the fact that West Germany has become associated with pacifist tendencies in the Alliance, for in the past it has been the fear of German militarism that most limited the Federal Republic's options. Both the formal limitations of treaties and the informal constraints of suspicion (in both East and West) reinforced a self-imposed sense of caution in the definition and articulation of West German security policy. As Willy Brandt and others have observed, it is novel indeed to hear complaints about Germans marching for peace.

None the less, popular opposition to defence policy is hardly new to post-war West Germany. Since the inception of the Federal Republic, West Germans have conducted a continuing debate over the necessity, role and control of its military institutions. Rearmament and accession to NATO opened the first phase of the debate, involving not only a recalcitrant public but also substantial sectors of the business community who feared that establishment of the Bundeswehr (Federal armed forces) would interfere with the labour and capital necessary for economic recovery.[1] With the acceptance of NATO and the Bundeswehr, attention turned to the task of integrating the military in the democratic political order. In fact, the task of reconciling military traditions with democracy continues to the present; it was the subject of Hans Apel's last official act as defence minister under the SDP/FDP coalition.

In the 1950s, opposition to the military went without saying for a population weary of war and weapons. Clear majorities opposed the draft that would be necessary for the creation of a German contingent in NATO, and the accession to NATO itself was opposed by the substantial plurality of 45% to 40%.[2] Although the Bundeswehr and NATO were eventually accepted, public attitudes towards the Bundeswehr remained ambivalent. As late as 1964, a near-majority of 48% held a 'mixed' or 'not good' opinion of it. By 1980, the total of mixed and poor opinions had declined to 43% (having reached the 50% level in 1969 and 1971).[3] Support for conscription rose steadily: to 58% by 1976 — a considerable increase in view of the clear majority who originally opposed it. But these figures are probably attributable more to deteriorating economic conditions and job prospects than to any fundamental change in attitudes towards the military.[4]

If the foregoing reveals only a grudging acceptance of the military as an institution, additional polls none the less suggest that the West German public considers it a necessary one. Polls in the late 1970s show that large majorities (89% in 1979) felt that the Bundeswehr 'makes peace more secure', while less than 10% considered it a 'threat to détente' or a 'danger to peace'.[5] The perceived importance of the Bundeswehr in 'current times and in the present world situation' has always been high and has increased recently.

In summary, West Germans reveal an understandable ambivalence towards military institutions, but the perceived need for the Bundeswehr has been stable and high. As we shall see, there is also strong support for alliance in NATO. The West German population may be sceptical of the military, but it has hardly been overcome by a 'pacifist' wave.

Threat perception and national priorities

West German polls on the fear of war and the Soviet threat provide clear documentation of the course of East-West relations since World War II. Two separate polls, one asking if West Germans felt 'threatened by the Russians', and a second asking if war is 'probable/possible' in the next three years, have been conducted regularly since 1952. Their results show a steady decline both in the sense of threat and in the fear of war until the early 1970s, since when both have gradually increased.[6] The long-run trend was interrupted in 1962, 1965 and 1980, when war expectations in particular rose sharply. (In 1980, threat perception and fear of war had reached the highest levels since the 1950s.)

But, as in other countries, crises appear to have only a temporary effect on threat perceptions. After all three occasions, fear of war returned quickly to the historical trend. Strong public concern for national security appears to result only in the wake of major crises. In West Germany, fear of war receded twenty points only a year after the events in Afghanistan; and in a poll conducted for the US government, fear of Soviet military attack was approximately the same in March 1981 as it had been in May 1979.[7]

West German opinion, like that of other NATO countries, is concerned more with domestic problems than with national security or foreign policy issues. Since 1961, studies conducted during national election campaigns have documented a drop in the priority accorded to defence. Concern for old-age security and price stability have consistently ranked highest, while concern for military security dropped from its 1961 peak to *lowest* place in 1971. Although defence concerns increased during the 1970s, they remained a lower priority than other issues, even in the tense atmosphere of 1980.[8] It is therefore not surprising that defence concerns have had little impact on election results. In general, German voters have been influenced more by their party ties, the qualities of the candidates, and domestic issues.[9]

The defence budget

Surveys reviewed in previous sections suggest that the impact of West German opinion is likely to be intermittent. In general, threat perception and concern for security are low except at times of crisis, and domestic problems have come to dominate public opinion and elections. Yet an indirect impact on policy is inevitable: in West Germany, as in other countries, a policy of budgetary restraint means that higher spending on defence implies sacrifice elsewhere in the budget. The question of distributional fairness takes on particular significance in light of the fact that the Schmidt/Genscher government foundered on the question of where and how much to cut the budget, and the duration of the Kohl/Genscher government may well hinge on how it deals with this very same issue.

Polls indicate that West Germans have increasingly taken the view that the defence budget should remain at the same level. Support for increased defence spending has declined slightly, while there has been a steep fall in sentiment to cut defence spending: from a peak of 41% in 1967, the percentage favouring a cut in defence declined to about one-fourth of those polled in 1978, and the tensions of 1979-80 have reduced the number even further.

The trend in preferences for a stable defence budget is interrupted by crisis periods. Between 1967 and 1969, and again between 1978 and 1980, a decline in those favouring defence cuts was in fact accompanied by a jump in those favouring increases (in both cases by a margin of about 10% each way). However, as might be expected from polls on threat perception, such fluctuations are short-lived.

The preference of West Germans for a stable defence budget is probably a result of several influences. Certainly attitudes resemble those towards the military in general: no outright rejection, but little enthusiasm either. Interestingly, opinions on defence spending also correspond to views of the military balance during the 1970s. About one-third of the public in a number of polls saw the Soviet Union (or Warsaw Pact) as superior in military strength, but considerable numbers (between 35% and 45%) saw the blocs as about equal, with a minority perceiving the United States (or NATO) as superior. In sum, about 45-65% of West Germans see the Western bloc as equal to or stronger than the Eastern. Coupled with the fact that 50-75% actually prefer parity (at least in the US-Soviet balance), assessments of the military balance provide little motivation to increase spending for defence.[10]

Of course, worry over possible cuts in popular domestic programmes is potentially the most significant influence on public opinion at a time of increasing budgetary stringency. West Germany is no different in this regard from other countries surveyed here. When faced with a choice, survey respondents rank defence at the top of the list of government programmes that should be cut if necessary. Defence spending remained a favoured target of cuts even in the wake of increased tensions in 1980. And while other programmes are hardly 'untouchable' in public opinion, the single largest category of public spending, transfers to individuals, is also the most protected in public opinion.[11] Thus, while there is sentiment to maintain a stable defence budget when surveys pose the issue in the abstract, public priorities suggest that continued budgetary retrenchment will present West German politicians with some difficult choices between defence spending and civilian spending.

Nuclear weapons, arms control and strategy

Given the geographical position of the Federal Republic, the failure of deterrence *or* arms control would present unpleasant futures: complete destruction or increasing uncertainty in the midst of the growing sophistication, if not number, of theatre nuclear forces. Yet despite recent attention to new weapons deployments and the precariousness of deterrence, West German public opinion is by no means as clear as might be inferred from the visibility of popular protest.

Reaction to the neutron weapon has been most negative. In two 1981 surveys, West Germans opposed the stationing of neutron weapons in the Federal Republic by a margin of 57% to 25% (March), and opposed their production and stationing by a margin of 54% to 45% (October).[12]

Opinions on the stationing of medium-range missiles are less clearcut. When confronted in May 1981 with a question on the 'stationing of American missiles . . . , for example in the Federal Republic', only 29% responded that they 'would welcome that', while 39% said they 'would not welcome that'.[13] The wording of this question is hardly ideal; one wonders under what conditions, if any, nuclear weapons can be considered 'welcome'. And, in fact, when the wording is varied, opinions on medium-range missiles change. In the May 1981 poll cited above, West Germans were asked if the NATO decision to 'station American medium-range missiles, for example in the Federal Republic, *to counterbalance Russian* medium-range missiles, should be prevented'. While 37% agreed that the NATO deployment should be prevented, 39% felt that it should not be prevented.[14] While a considerable percentage remain undecided in each of these surveys, clearly the reference to Soviet actions in the second question has reversed the negative sentiments revealed in other questions.

A similar effect occurs when surveys mention the negotiation part of NATO's dual-track decision of 1979. In a survey in October 1981 for the weekly *Spiegel*, West Germans favoured the deployment of medium-range missiles when they were informed that the NATO decision 'also proposed negotiations with the Soviet Union, with the goal of completely or partially forgoing [deployment] if agreement on arms limitation can be reached'.[15] This poll, however, indicated a decline in support for deployment since May 1981, when a similar 'dual-track' query had been posed by Allensbach; then respondents had favoured the deploy/negotiate decision by 53% to 20%.[16]

From the surveys on the neutron bomb and on NATO's medium-range missile decision, it seems clear that West German attitudes towards nuclear weapons, though hardly warm, are none the less sensitive to mention of NATO commitments, to the presumed need to balance Soviet deployments and to the intention to seek negotiated limitations of the systems.

A similar pattern emerges in the public's reaction to NATO's strategy of flexible response. Since 1976, surveys have posed a battery of questions that 'test' the public's attitudes towards nuclear defence. As shown in Table 8, an average of 60% favour 'defending the national territory' from attack, 'and this willingness drops only slightly when respondents are asked about defence 'even if the war were to be fought for the most part on the territory of the Federal Republic'. However, when respondents are asked to consider the use of nuclear weapons in defence of the national territory, support drops precipitously.

This attitude is hardly surprising given the consequences of a nuclear exchange on West German soil. Yet some West Germans are apparently willing to consider it when the question is worded to include references to the Soviet Union. In October 1981, far less than a majority of West

Table 8   West German attitudes towards nuclear defence

Q: 'Do you think that the Federal Republic should defend itself against an attack on its territory?'

	Yes %	No %	DK; NA %	N
July/Aug. 1976	62	15	23	1588
June/July 1977	59	19	22	1187
Dec./Jan. 1977–8	57	22	21	1913
Oct./Nov. 1979	57	20	23	1866
Feb./Mar. 1980	64	19	16	559

Q: 'Are you in favour of defending the Federal Republic against military attack even if the war were to be fought for the most part on the territory of the Federal Republic?'

	Yes %	No %	DK; NA %	N
Dec./Jan. 1977–8	57	38	5	1913
Oct./Nov. 1979	50	29	22	1866
Feb./Mar. 1980	53	31	17	559

Q: 'In case of war, NATO has, among others, atomic weapons at its disposal. Are you in favour of military defence, even if atomic weapons have to be employed on the territory of the Federal Republic?'

	Yes %	No %	DK; NA %	N
Dec./Jan. 1977–78	19	61	20	1913
Oct./Nov. 1979	15	66	20	1866
Feb./Mar. 1980	15	71	14	559

Source: Provided by Press and Information Office, Federal Ministry of Defence. Surveys by INFAS.

Germans (38%) opposed the use of nuclear weapons when the survey question referred to a 'Soviet attack [overrunning] NATO conventional forces' or to 'Soviet forces [using] nuclear weapons first in attacking Western Europe'. Although the anti-nuclear movement in West Germany has been among the most visible in Western Europe, this percentage is lower than that for Italy and the Netherlands, and not much different from that for Britain and France.

To summarize, West German opinion on nuclear weapons cannot be characterized simply. Certainly the population is unenthusiastic about nuclear weapons in general and about the neutron weapon in particular. Yet the public is less negative when deployment, or even use, of nuclear weapons is mentioned as a *response* to Soviet deployments or actions or when arms control efforts are included in the question. Although anti-nuclear demonstrations in West Germany are surely evidence of a substantial, well-organized minority, opinion surveys indicate that at the same time there exists a not inconsiderable reservoir of support for NATO's package of deployment and negotiation.

NATO and the United States

As relations with the East relaxed as a result of Nixon's détente and Brandt's *Ostpolitik*, the Federal Republic's 'Western policy' appeared more and more successful. Security and economic growth were assured by the Western orientation, and if reunification remained a distant prospect, détente had at least achieved a modicum of human contact and economic exchange.

The Western anchor of West German foreign policy enjoyed overwhelming public support after the initial scepticism of the 1950s. One survey question reveals the extent of support for NATO membership: sentiment to withdraw from the Alliance has never exceeded a tiny fraction of public opinion, while support for continued membership has remained steady at slightly less than 80% of the population (Table 9). Further, an average of 70% of West Germans continue to believe that 'NATO is essential' to the Federal Republic's security. The sharp drop in this percentage between 1980 and 1981 (1982 figures are not yet available) was perhaps a response to the belligerent tone of the new American administration. The data in Table 9 indicate no similar increase in sentiment to withdraw from NATO, and other polls show that 'neutralist' sentiment has not increased above its historical average of about 35%. In fact, the desire to 'remain neutral', rather than be 'militarily allied to the United States', was lower in

Table 9   West German support for NATO (%)

Q: 'What do you personally think: Should the Federal Republic remain a member of NATO, or should it withdraw?'

	Remain	Withdraw	Undecided	Uninformed on NATO
Dec. 1955	24	4	2	70
1969	79	4	17	—
1971	71	5	9	15
1979	78	2	7	13
May 1981	78	6	NA	NA

Sources: 1955: Richard Merritt and Donald Puchala, eds, *Western European Perspectives on International Affairs* (New York, Praeger, 1968), p. 345. 1969–79: Federal Press and Information Office, *Dreissig Jahre NATO* (Bonn, 1981), mimeographed, p. 34; and *Capital* (August, 1981), p. 90. The 1969–79 sources reproduce surveys by Allensbach.

1981 than it had been earlier (27% in 1981, as against 42% in 1961 and 1973).[17]

Moreover, neutralist sentiments, at least throughout 1981, were hardly a dominant segment of opinion, certainly no more than in other West European countries. The current state of the Alliance suggests that it is American policies, and not the Alliance itself, that are in dispute. Most striking, polls conducted for the American government reveal that in West Germany the balance of favourable over unfavourable views of the United States dropped by almost forty points between 1978 and 1982 (although favourable ratings still dominate). A similar drop has occurred in West German confidence in the ability of the United States 'to deal responsibly with world problems'.[18]

In view of these data, it is not surprising that West German public opinion has grown cautious in its evaluation of American foreign policy. For example, in 1981 a substantial minority (35%) felt that 'it is no longer possible to subordinate ourselves to American leadership in everything', although 48% believed that West Germany must 'continue to be firmly on the side of the United States'.[19] In another poll in 1981, West Germans appeared more willing to back American policy than did public opinion in other West European countries, where a much higher percentage prefer that their countries 'stay out of

US–Soviet disputes' rather than 'side with the United States'. This view was taken by 65% of Italian respondents, 64% of British, 58% of French and 54% of Dutch, as against 41% of West Germans.[20] Although West Germany's interests in good relations with the East are arguably more vital than those of its NATO neighbours, West German public opinion is none the less comparatively more willing to pursue those interests together with the United States.

Summary and conclusions

Our review of West German public opinion suggests several conclusions. Most important, the polls indicate little evidence of 'pacifist', 'neutralist' or 'anti-American' majorities. West Germans long ago accepted the necessity of the Bundeswehr and the NATO Alliance, and public support for these institutions of security policy remains high. Feelings towards the defence budget and nuclear weapons are more mixed, even negative by some standards, but they hardly reveal a total rejection of Alliance postures. Finally, American leadership has come under question, but apparently less so than in other NATO countries, and in the event the margin of anti-Americanism is not overwhelming or even of majority proportions.

To be sure, the surveys indicate that NATO is not without its problems in the Federal Republic. So long as budgets remain tight, for example, the political room for additional defence spending is limited. Moreover, failure of arms control negotiations would presumably add to existing uncertainties in the population. Such political problems are not peculiar to the Federal Republic.

It must be conceded that opposition to security policy has been more visible in the Federal Republic than in other countries, leading many to suppose that it is less important *how many* people hold opinions than *who* holds them. The young and educated, it has been argued, are both better equipped to mobilize in opposition and more disposed to do so because of their lesser attachment to traditional foreign policy orientations.[21] And it may be that party positions are growing apart once again after many years of a centrist consensus on defence; here the focus is the Social Democratic Party.

Not a great deal of research has been done on generational or party attitudes.[22] None the less, existing evidence suggests that societal divisions are not as clear-cut as simple generational theories or presumed partisan motivations would indicate. For example, research by the American government reveals that nuclear pacifism is stronger among conservatives than among other partisan groups;[23] other surveys suggest that flexible response is rejected by older West Germans as well as by the young. The underlying sources of West German opinion on defence issues are more complex than simple labels would make out.[24]

8 The United States

When Ronald Reagan became president in January 1981, the American public was more concerned about national security than at any time since the Korean war. Although public opinion had been growing increasingly tense since the mid-1970s, events in Afghanistan and Iran stimulated unprecedented fear and pessimism: in 1980, 83% of the public considered war likely, an increase from 47% in 1978. Further, Americans were angered and frustrated by the events of 1979 and 1980. Reviewing a number of polls in 1981, the opinion analysts Daniel Yankelovich and Larry Kaagan reported that Americans felt 'bullied', 'humiliated' and 'outgunned'.[1]

Given the mood of the country, it is not surprising that Ronald Reagan found widespread support for his programme of building up defence forces, delaying arms control and retreating from the last remnants of détente with the Soviet Union. And, given European sensitivity about nuclear weapons and defence spending, it is also not surprising that relations between the United States and its European allies, already strained under Jimmy Carter, took a turn for the worse soon after the inauguration of President Reagan. White House officials accused Europeans of 'contemptible' values and questioned the patriotism of some European politicians. By the beginning of 1982, fully 80% of the American public believed that the European allies were not 'supporting the United States as much as they should', and almost half believed that the Europeans had actually 'worked against' the United States during the Polish crisis.[2]

Yet just as it appeared that Atlantic relations would reach breaking-point, official policy and public opinion in the United States began to shift. Perhaps most surprising was the emergence of an American counterpart to European anti-nuclear movements. Reacting to the extensive procurement plans of the Reagan administration and to talk of limited nuclear exchanges (both a continuation from previous administrations), anti-nuclear activists coalesced in a number of groups. By 1982, the movement found considerable support in local and state governing bodies as well as in the US Congress, and freeze motions fared well in the November elections. The pressure to begin arms control initiatives was matched by similar demands to reduce the magnitude and cost of the five-year defence spending plan.

Uncertainties about defence policy were not confined to the public or to the President's (liberal) Democratic critics. The administration itself demonstrated substantial flexibility when the time came to implement some of its policies. The MX missile underwent considerable delay as opposition from within the President's own party forced the Pentagon to consider basing plans that would not disturb the environment in important Republican states of the West. Despite his anti-Soviet rhetoric, President Reagan also felt it necessary to keep his pledge to farmers to remove the grain embargo. He was forced, further, to accept demands from both parties that the defence programme be slowed to avoid higher budget deficits or further cuts in popular domestic programmes. To this list of domestic compromises must be added the effort to assuage European concerns: accelerated arms control initiatives at all levels, relaxation of pressure to achieve the 3% real increase in defence spending, and 'agreement to disagree' on the question of restricting trade with the East.

The reasons for the change in the administration's tone certainly included a desire to maintain Alliance solidarity at a time when European governments were under domestic pressure (this may be a relatively rare case of European public opinion influencing American policy). It is also true that the administration has been forced to deal with important interests within its own party, especially on the grain embargo, the MX basing plan and the defence budget.

Reagan's programme[3] *and the public's reponse*

Given the ideological tradition of American foreign policy, it is perhaps not surprising that public opinion shares the Reagan administration's concern for the Soviet threat. Yet the margin of negative sentiments and fear is startling all the same. In a 1982 poll for Louis Harris, the following results were obtained: 84% see the Soviet Union as a 'threat to the security of the United States'; 63% think that the Soviet Union will attack the United States during the next forty years; 69% think that the Russians would not hesitate to use nuclear arms 'if they were desperate enough'; and 49% view the Soviet Union as an 'outright enemy'.[4] Although these questions are not identical with corresponding questions described in earlier chapters (the wording is also somewhat leading), it is apparent that American fears of the Soviet Union are greater than those of Europeans.

However, there is also some differentiation of opinion on the Soviet threat. Despite the largely negative views listed above, other polls suggest a less fearful public. Thus, only 34% of American opinion believes that the Soviet Union 'seeks global domination and will risk a major war to achieve that domination if it can't be achieved by other means'.[5] Furthermore, the public seems willing to attempt to overcome differences with the Soviet Union in order to solve important bilateral and international problems: 90% would favour negotiations on energy problems; 88% would favour negotiations on pollution problems; and 72% favour an expansion of US-Soviet trade.[6] In summary, American opinion bears some resemblance to European: little affection or confidence in the Soviet system, but a desire to reduce tensions where possible.

Of course, these 1982 surveys may also reflect a shift in the administration's own tone in dealing with the Soviet Union. President Reagan has moved to open negotiations on arms control matters. Furthermore, these polls come *after* two Reagan budgets and the substantial additions to the defence effort that these will entail. Finally, the public has no doubt relaxed somewhat after the near hysteria of the Iran hostage crisis and the Soviet invasion of Afghanistan.

The change is also visible in the public's assessment of the military balance with the Soviet Union. Reagan, of course, has made American inferiority a major theme of his defence statements, and early in his administration public opinion closely agreed with this view. During 1980, the view that the Soviet Union was superior in military strength increased dramatically, to well over 50%; less than 10% thought that the United States was superior; and about 30% thought that the two superpowers were about equal in strength. However, the perception of inferiority eroded rapidly: by January 1983, less than 40% saw the Soviet Union as superior and just under a majority had come to believe that parity existed (although there continues to be little belief that the United States is superior).

The calmer assessment of the military balance is no doubt a result of declining tensions. And, of course, the substantial sums appropriated for defence during the last several years may have contributed to the feeling that the balance is being 'corrected'. Nevertheless, the President has stubbornly insisted that recent expenditures are not alone sufficient to correct the military balance, and he has continued to argue that the United States is inferior. Thus, change in the public's assessment of the military balance is in spite of, rather than because of, the President's arguments.

In fact, it is also possible that, like some West Europeans, Americans see the defence increases as an overreaction. In the following section we discuss this issue in terms of budgetary trade-offs. Here it is useful to point out that, while the public had come to see trends in the military balance as adverse to the United States, a substantial minority continued to perceive a situation of parity, even during the crisis period of 1980-1. Further, when asked to state what they *prefer*, the same substantial minority (never less than 40%) favour equality in US–Soviet military strength. Thus, to the extent that the Reagan defence programme evokes images of an attempt to achieve superiority, there is the potential for opposition among those who prefer strategic parity.

None the less, in general, American public opinion tends to support the broad thrust of the Reagan defence policy. The Soviet Union is seen as threatening, and although views of the American military position have improved, large numbers of survey respondents still see the United States as inferior and would prefer that the country seek superiority. There are signs of ambivalence, since the public seems to favour negotiations with the Soviet Union, and in any case there is substantial sentiment that military parity is the desirable goal of defence policy.

Ambivalence is much more pronounced when we turn to the issue of *using* military force, an important consideration in view of the administration's emphasis on global force projection. There is some general evidence that the 'Vietnam syndrome' has receded; a standard survey battery designed to measure the degree of isolationism in American opinion showed a sharp increase in internationalist sentiment in 1980 (to 61%), and in any case there has been gradually increasing internationalism since the low point of 1974, when only 41% were classified as 'internationalists'.[7]

Of course, willingness to use force abroad is another matter, and here the public shows more caution. True, its willingness to come to the assistance of the Western allies (and Japan) has shown a sharp rise in recent years. The percentage favouring the 'use of force' to defend the allies had been growing during the 1970s, and it surpassed 60% in 1980. When asked directly if they favoured using American troops in the defence of Western Europe, 65% of respondents answered favourably in 1982, an increase from 39% in 1974 and 54% in 1978.[8]

However, these survey questions present both clear threats (invasion of Europe or Japan) and interests traditionally regarded as vital. When other geographical areas are mentioned as possible theatres of American military action, opinion is less certain. For example, Richman reviews a series of past polls regarding American military options in Zaire (1978), Somalia (1978) and El Salvador (1981). They show that in none of these situations would more than two-fifths of the public favour military action, and even then the responses are quite cautious: approximately two-fifths favoured 'non-combat advisors', one-fifth favoured 'combat advisors' and one-tenth would send US troops. In the autumn of 1982, majorities opposed the selling of military equipment or the granting of military aid to Third World countries.[9]

Final evidence of the public's selective approach to the potential use of American troops is revealed in a further series of polls. Asked in 1980 if American troops should be used in the case of 'Soviet invasion', 60% favoured defending Western Europe (54% for West Berlin) and 64% the Persian Gulf, but only 36% were in favour for Yugoslavia and 20% for South Korea. When local threats are posed, the public is even more opposed to the use of troops: 35% in the case of Israel (if overrun by an Arab country) and 22% in the case of Saudi Arabia (if overrun by another Middle Eastern country).[10] These polls led one

State Department analyst to conclude in 1982: 'Although polls have shown a sharp increase since the mid-1970s in the public's support for military means to enhance US security, concern about becoming embroiled in "another Vietnam situation" remains a significant constraint on the public's willingness to intervene in situations which do not appear to threaten US vital interests.'[11]

Guns or butter?

In his 1982 Posture Statement, the Secretary of Defense, Caspar Weinberger, was confident that the American public would support the President's policies: 'Fifteen months ago the American people gave Ronald Reagan the mandate to lead our nation. That mandate emphasized the strengthening of America.'[12]

Until 1982, Weinberger's assessment of the public's support for a defence build-up was certainly true. In fact, throughout the 1970s there had been a gradual shift in American opinion in the direction of support for increased defence spending. After the extreme tensions of 1979 and 1980, this support reached unprecedented levels. Not since the Korean war had such a large percentage of survey respondents found that defence spending was 'too little': 51% of the standard Gallup survey in 1981. Even higher margins (65% in January 1981) favoured increases when the question asked simply if defence spending should be 'increased, decreased or kept the same'.[13] The erosion of this sentiment is therefore all the more remarkable. By January 1983, opposition to defence spending (spending is 'too much') had risen to levels not seen since the early 1970s. In a CBS/*New York Times* survey, only 11% thought that defence spending was 'too little', and 48% thought it 'too much'.

We have already suggested some of the reasons for this decline in support for the defence budget. Tensions deriving from the international situation, while not totally absent, had lessened considerably with the resolution of the Iran hostage crisis. The Reagan defence increases adopted in 1981 and 1982 make (or foresee) substantial additions or improvements to American weaponry, perhaps another cause for a growth in the feeling that the defence budget has 'had enough'.

None the less, it is equally clear that concern for cuts in domestic programmes has also caused the public to reconsider the cost of increasing military strength. In fact, during the period of strengthening sentiment for defence increases, there was never a shift in the public's basic priorities. In a yearly survey throughout the 1970s, for example, the percentage who thought defence was getting 'too little' did not change much, perhaps because it was posed as part of a series of questions in which competing domestic programmes (such as law and order, the environment and education) were also mentioned. The latter programmes far outweighed defence among the public's priorities. The classic 'most important problem' question produced a similar concentration on domestic priorities, especially the state of the economy.[14] Asked directly whether the country should attend to its own problems or think more in international terms, the response has always had an inward-looking emphasis.

Concern for a 'guns/butter' trade-off is also evident in surveys bearing directly on the Reagan budgetary strategy. For example, polls for ABC/*Washington Post* asked if the Reagan defence increases were 'just right', went 'too far', or 'did not go far enough'. In April of 1981, just after President Reagan's initial budgetary pronouncements, a clear majority thought that the defence increases were 'just right', and only 17% thought that they went 'too far'. By March 1982, however, after the first round of civilian spending cuts had been legislated and a second round proposed, 41% believed that the increases went 'too far'.[15]

Public sentiment for cutting defence (or halting the proposed increases) has grown as the problems of budgetary deficits have brought the issue of trade-offs to the popular agenda. Asked by CBS/*New York Times* how budget deficits could be reduced, 45% were willing to consider cuts in defence in March 1982, an increase from 33% two months earlier. In May 1982, 48% favoured cutting defence to reduce the deficit, versus 31% who were willing to cut benefits for the poor (Table 10). By January 1983 (after the proposal of a third round of cuts in civil spending), the preference for cutting defence had reached 68%.[16]

It is interesting that neither the Congress nor the President seems willing to take advantage of a surprising finding of public opinion

Table 10   American views on reducing the deficit (%)

Q: 'To reduce the size of the federal deficit, would you be willing or
not willing to:'

	Willing		Not Willing	
	3/82	5/82	3/82	5/82
(1) ... eliminate the federal income tax cut planned for next year [for July, 1983]	53	55	32	27
(2) ... reduce the size of the federal income tax cut planned for next July	59		28	
(3) ... have the government reduce *proposed* spending on military and defence programmes	49	48	41	44
(4) ... postpone cost-of-living increases in social security benefits [reduce scheduled cost-of-living increases]	37	31	57	61
(5) ... have the government reduce *proposed* spending on programmes for the poor	29	31	63	61
(6) ... reduce social security payments for people who retire before age 65		26		67

Note: Wording in brackets denotes May 1982 wording.
Source: CBS/*New York Times*.

surveys, the willingness to forgo tax cuts to help reduce the budget
deficit. As Table 10 shows, there is a close split in public opinion
on these issues, but it is clear that revocation of planned tax cuts
is a more popular option than cutting non-defence programmes, and
surprisingly the survey also shows it to be a more popular option than
cutting defence.

Yet it was precisely at the time of these surveys (during 1982)
that the President and his supply-side supporters were most vehement
in their opposition to tax increases (although the President did agree
to some non-income-tax 'revenue enhancements'). If this insistence
continues, Congressional sentiment to cut defence is likely to remain
strong. Although substantial increases have been appropriated, in
the future the American politics of defence should look more like the
European than many would have thought possible in 1980 or 1981.

Nuclear weapons and arms control

It is somewhat ironic that anti-nuclear sentiments in Western Europe should be equated with 'anti-Americanism', for the American public is actually quite receptive to nuclear arms control. As already noted, a large segment of public opinion prefers parity in the military balance, perhaps a reflection of the emphasis on 'parity' or 'essential equivalence' in government strategic and arms control policy over the last decade. As regards the US–Soviet strategic balance, few survey respondents find that the United States is ahead, but the remainder – since about the mid-1970s – has been divided between the view that the Soviet Union is superior and the view that the superpowers are about equal in nuclear strength. In a Harris survey in May 1982, 47% found that the superpowers were equal in nuclear strength, as against 34% who thought the United States was 'weaker' than the Soviet Union.[17]

Like West Europeans, Americans oppose the use of nuclear weapons. For example, we saw previously that up to 65% of the American public were prepared in 1981–2 to 'use force' or 'send troops' to defend Western Europe from Soviet attack. But when asked (in 1981) if the United States should use nuclear weapons to defend Western Europe, only 29–37% were in favour.[18]

Support for the general idea of freezing nuclear arsenals is extremely high. In a large number of polls conducted by Louis Harris, NBC/ *Washington Post* and CBS/*New York Times*, support for a variety of 'freeze' formulations never dropped below 70% during 1982. Polls describing a freeze on 'production, storage and use' of nuclear weapons were favoured by 70%, and a poll suggesting a one-third cut in the arsenals of the two superpowers found 82% support. The public also favours continuation of the START process by wide margins.[19]

Yet before concluding that the political impact of public opinion will be great, one should note that the public's hostility and suspicion towards the Soviet Union also colours arms control opinions. Thus 78% of the public believe that 'the Soviets only want agreements when they can gain an advantage'; and 75% are sceptical that the Soviets will keep their end of agreements. When possible Soviet cheating is mentioned, support for freeze proposals drops to 18%, and only 26% support a freeze if 'the United States would have to freeze first'.

Finally, in a poll posing two alternatives, 42% of the public would support a freeze unconditionally, but 54% prefer to 'build for a strong position to negotiate arms control'.[20]

Of course, few of these surveys describe realistic possibilities in any ongoing negotiation. Yet it is significant that the questions should be posed in the first place, for they reflect the tone of arms control debates in the United States. President Reagan has defended his defence programme and his halting movement towards arms control with negative references to the Soviet system in general and by concentrating on the themes of cheating and Soviet strength. Given the basic level of suspicion of Americans for the Soviet Union, these concerns are likely to weaken the political impact of otherwise favourable attitudes towards arms control.

The United States and Western Europe

Despite the considerable differences that have troubled the Alliance during the past several years, our review of American opinion suggests that by 1983 opinion in Europe and America had many things in common. For example, as earlier chapters have shown, there is less sentiment in Europe for actually cutting the defence budget than for holding it stable to avoid a trade-off that would affect civilian programmes. This chapter shows that Americans have also lost their enthusiasm for increasing defence spending as the crisis atmosphere of recent years has receded and the budgetary implications have become clear. Further, anti-nuclear sentiment in European countries is not so much a reflection of a general anti-defence, pacifist wave as a reaction to specific defence policies (war-fighting) of member governments. The same aversion to the *use* of nuclear weapons is found in the United States, and certainly protest against nuclear weapons has grown there as well.

Significantly, Americans, like Europeans, continue to support the Alliance, despite the bitter rhetoric that has sometimes characterized recent Atlantic discussions. And despite the feeling that the NATO allies had not supported the United States on a number of issues, throughout 1982 Americans continued to support the stationing of American troops in Europe; opposition to the European troop presence never rose to the levels of the Mansfield period (Table 11).

Table 11   American support for stationing of US troops in Europe (%)

Q: 'As you probably know, the United States now has substantial military forces stationed in Europe for defence purposes. Under present circumstances, do you think the commitment of forces in Europe should be increased, kept at the present level, reduced or ended altogether?'

	Increased	Present Level	Reduced	Ended
Jan. 1974	3	52	25	12
April 1978	9	59	14	9
Sept. 1979	16	53	12	11
Feb. 1982	16	50	10	11

Source: Surveys by Gallup, as reported in Ellen Malone and Alvin Richman, 'American Attitudes on the Building and Use of Military Power', materials presented to the Convention of the International Studies Association, Cincinnati, Ohio, March 1982.

Of course, one must be cautious as regards the depth and permanence of American public opinion. Like American foreign policy generally, it can fluctuate between extreme retrenchment and withdrawal and enthusiastic commitment. Public and government alike appear to alternate between a desire to compete with the Soviet Union and a recognition of the material and, increasingly, technological limits of that competition. Thus, current signs of caution in American opinion may be only a temporary phenomenon, to be erased if a future crisis once again focuses the public's attention on the Soviet Union.

The divergence that exists between the interests and perspectives of the United States and those of the European countries suggests two things about the way in which public opinion in America and Europe will manifest itself. The first, quite simply, is that American opinion is likely to fluctuate more strongly than European in response to real or imagined threats from the Soviet Union; in this case, we would expect periodic repetition of US-European disagreement. Second, American opinion on security questions is likely to be more sensitive to external events than to pragmatic, domestic considerations; whereas European opinion (barring a major crisis in Europe) is likely to be determined more by budgetary preoccupations or party differences than by the level of international tensions. Whether these differences will lead to a fundamental crisis in the Atlantic Alliance is a much broader question, addressed in the final chapter of this paper.

9 Conclusions

Stability and change

During the past three years, normal irritations and tactical disagreements in the Western Alliance have been superseded by a much more fundamental concern. Many observers on both sides of the Atlantic have begun to ask if the public continues to support the established features of security policy. Labels such as 'pacifism', 'neutralism' or 'anti-Americanism' may be oversimplifications, but the fact that they have become almost standard items in the Western vernacular indicates their widespread appeal.

Our review of public opinion suggests that these terms are not appropriate descriptions of public views in Western Europe (just as labels such as ('hawkish' or 'hard-line' would be misleading simplifications of the views of the American public of 1983). Previous chapters show that public support for NATO remains high in all the European member states. Nor is there any sign that the legitimacy and utility of military institutions have been rejected as a matter of principle, as the 'pacifist' label would suggest. In fact, even on the issue of nuclear weapons, public opinion is not nearly as hostile as is commonly assumed: the British and French publics continue to support their national deterrents, and even the Dutch and West Germans, although more polarized than their NATO partners by the INF issue, are sensitive to arguments concerning the need for nuclear weapons as a deterrent or as part of a commitment to NATO.

This finding is important, for it shows that both governments and outside observers must go beyond simple labels in seeking to understand popular views of defence policies. Equally significant, the considerable continuities in public opinion indicate that popular reaction to the many changes in the post-war environment has been much less dramatic than is often assumed. It was common during the 1970s to argue that developments in international politics and economics would produce changes in attitudes approaching a reasonable definition of 'pacifism'. In particular, scholars such as Seyom Brown, Edward Morse and, most prominently, Robert Keohane and Joseph Nye argued that military force was becoming increasingly irrelevant or dysfunctional in solving the problems on the agenda of international politics. To the extent that military power had been attenuated and new issues had come to dominate this agenda, defence policy would have to take a back seat (or at least accept a lower priority) to non-military instruments of security policy.[1]

If mass publics were in tune with such arguments, public support for the instruments of defence policy could be expected to decline. Where the use of force in minor disputes risked escalation, when the achievement of superpower parity presented a security 'stalemate', and when other 'non-military' issues called for attention, could public opinion be expected to move in any direction other than away from support for the military dimension of security policy?

The impact of this line of reasoning seems to have faded in the wake of recent international crises, and the actions of British and French forces during the past five years hardly indicate a total lack of utility for the use of force. In the light of these recent events, the comparative absence of pacifist sentiment in public opinion is perhaps not surprising. Despite the emergence of superpower parity, economic interdependence and a 'new agenda' in international relations, attitudes towards the military aspects of the Alliance and military force in general remain positive. This suggests that the staying power of the consensus surrounding the need for standing military forces has been underestimated in recent writing on the subject.

This is not to say that the Alliance does not face the problem of legitimizing its policies. If the foregoing chapters do not reveal pacifism, they do point to problems of present or future political conflict in many (if not all) member states. The first and most divisive of these is the issue of nuclear force modernization. True, our review of opinion polls indicates that nuclear weapons as such are not generally rejected, and even on the question of intermediate nuclear modernization public opinion is about evenly divided. None the less, the experience of the past several years suggests that it is precisely by the intensity and visibility of the opposition that NATO's decision has been called into question. Given the real difficulty of designing a deterrence strategy in an age of US–Soviet parity, this opposition may wane, but it is unlikely to disappear.

A second source of concern for NATO governments is the level of positive public support for defence budgets. This is true of public opinion on both sides of the Atlantic. When broader societal priorities are considered, public opinion generally opts for 'butter' rather than 'guns'. The fact that support for defence spending is lukewarm is particularly troubling for NATO governments because it comes at a time when conventional alternatives to nuclear weapons are being sought by many. In the United States, moreover, budget constraints may combine with dissatisfaction with the European partners to produce a more isolationist security orientation.

Thus, the third problem in public opinion is all the more sensitive: the decline in the image of the United States in Western Europe. True, it is difficult to say with certainty if the recent dip in attitudes towards America (visible in every country surveyed here) is permanent. It may be only a temporary phenomenon, but it is no less of a problem for that, for it comes at a time when Atlantic understanding is especially important if solutions to security issues are to be found.

'Explanations'

It is interesting that, in seeking to understand public scepticism of defence policies, governments have increasingly turned from 'pacifist' or 'neutralist' generalizations to more subtle explanations based on the nature of social changes that their societies have undergone over the past thirty years. Thus, political leaders — including Arthur Burns, the American ambassador in Bonn, and Hans-Dietrich Genscher, the West German foreign minister — have been arguing that the younger, 'successor' generation of their societies must be brought to understand the reasons for security policies: the need to deter Soviet power; the common traditions of the Western Alliance; and the fact of previous Soviet threats, as in Hungary, Czechoslovakia and East Germany. In each case, the politicians are suggesting that a new generation has emerged that is unaware of (or unreceptive to) traditional justifications for the Western Alliance and its policies, and they have accepted the need for governments to do a better job in explaining the foundations of Western security policy.[2]

Those who grew to maturity after World War II have been much more secure economically, politically and militarily. Unlike their elders, the post-war generations have not known extreme material deprivation or the bitterness of war. As a result, they are less likely to emphasize the 'older' values that placed primary importance on material concerns and national security.[3]

The political significance of this new generation is to be found not only in gradually changing values, but also in the fact that the young are much better educated than their elders. To the extent that political sophistication and interest in politics increase with education, the post-war generations are more likely to be mobilized and to participate effectively in political debates. Moreover, the search for consensus may be rendered more difficult by the participation of the new generations, since their values often place them outside the familiar partisan basis of existing political systems. The emergence and impact of the Green Party in West Germany illustrates this consensus problem.

Further, one is tempted to argue that the decline of the American image in Western Europe is due to generational change. Of course, the American image had already suffered as a result of the Vietnam and Watergate experiences, and the current disenchantment may simply reflect generational differences in the perception of the 'threat'. Yet to the extent that the decline in the American image is most pronounced among the young, it may also be due to a generational difference of a more fundamental nature: the fact that the older European generations that experienced the post-war economic miracle tended to emulate, if not explicitly accept, American values.

In some countries there may have been political and cultural convergence with the American model as well. In any event, anti-Americanism among the young may simply be a return to a historical European scepticism concerning the economic and cultural bases of American society.[4]

However appealing the generational argument, it probably does not explain differences in public opinion on all defence issues. For example, European opinion on the appropriate level of defence spending is less polarized than in other areas of security policy (although major increases are not generally favoured) and, to judge by fragmentary evidence, it does not appear to be clearly aligned on the basis of age.

An understanding of the politics of the defence budget requires an examination of the broader political constraints created by the growth of the modern welfare state during the post-war period. Welfare politics are quite distinct from theories of generational change, despite the common focus on the values of individual dignity and worth, because they embrace a far wider spectrum of political interests. For example, Harold and Margaret Sprout have argued that the growth of welfare spending and the corresponding decline in defence spending in the United Kingdom was an inevitable result of the extension of power to the working class. Edward Morse has applied substantially the same argument to increasing constraints on the French defence budget. In these analyses, political claims are not confined to a small segment of the population, such as the young, but are asserted by the broader mass of the population who received little in the way of budgetary favour in previous historical periods.[5]

Welfare policy, funded from the economic growth of the 1960s and 1970s, must now compete with the demands of external security, both in the East-West context and in the demands of the southern hemisphere for aid and trade. Thus, it is argued, the growth of the welfare state will lead to severe constraints on the ability of governments to allocate money to defence.[6]

The political and financial obligations of the welfare state are obvious reasons for the current lack of enthusiasm in Western Europe (and the United States!) for major increases in the defence budget. This constraint can be illustrated clearly through a final set of survey results. In 1979 and 1981, the Commission of the European Communities surveyed attitudes in all EC countries on a number of policy issues, including the question of strengthening defence and efforts to reduce income inequality (the questions were separate).[7] The results are straightforward: far more respondents favour the goal of reducing income inequality than favour the goal of strengthening defence. There is a partial exception. In the United Kingdom, and to some extent in West Germany and the Netherlands, the defence goal ranks close to the social goal of reducing inequality. Interestingly, the two polls also show some willingness on the part of the public to adjust to the recent recession — there is a decline between 1979 and 1981 in all but two countries in the percentage favouring the 'equality' question, perhaps a recognition of the scarcity of revenues to pursue social policies. Nevertheless, it is also significant that, during the period of growing international tensions between 1979 and 1981, there was not a uniform increase in respondents favouring strengthened defence. In France, Italy and Denmark there was some increase in sensitivity to defence needs, but not in the United Kingdom, West Germany or the Netherlands, and in any case the social priority remained dominant. These results confirm a conclusion drawn in each of the individual country studies reviewed in this paper: as a matter of political necessity, the defence budget cannot be treated differently from other government programmes, especially at a time of budgetary retrenchment.

Of course, the wide margins of public support for social goals also suggest an important point about the political nature of the budgetary constraint imposed by the modern welfare state: it is fundamentally different from the problem of the 'successor generation' described previously. After all, the major beneficiaries of the modern welfare state are the older, more established members of society: the aged (pensions), parents (family benefits) and those of working age (health insurance, unemployment protection).

If the political interests represented by the second group are different from those of the first group, it is natural to expect that the policy consequences will also be different. In fact, one would expect the second group's opposition to the defence budget to be less severe and more manageable. In the first place, their opposition to defence spending, although it may involve a larger number of people, is presumably based on short-run economic interest rather than opposition in principle. In fact, the older beneficiaries of the welfare state are probably more receptive to justifications for defence spending; they share the 'Cold War axioms' to a greater extent than the young. A second reason for the manageability of defence budget debates is that budgetary resources are divisible, and thus can be compromised or traded in a pattern of taking turns or stretching out. Such compromises are not easily achieved on issues where differences in opinion stem from value conflicts or fundamentally different perceptions of the threat.

If our interpretation of trends in public opinion is correct, it should be both a relief and a warning to Alliance governments. It is a relief because we have shown that the presence of serious public doubts about some defence policies has not led to a general collapse of support for the Alliance or its institutions. But there is also a warning, since our argument suggests that the resolution of one problem will not guarantee the resolution of other problems.

The distinction between budgetary and non-budgetary conflicts also suggests implications for the durability of defence policy debates. Budgetary problems will not disappear; the cluster of interests surrounding civilian programmes is unlikely to erode, and its composition will change only slowly. The potential for budgetary conflicts, therefore, is essentially constant and will be affected primarily by the relative abundance of budgetary resources. Non-budgetary conflicts, in contrast, can be stimulated by short-term events that affect wider NATO strategy.

A crisis in Atlantic relations?

A study of public opinion polls in Western Europe and the United States makes it much easier to identify what problems do *not* exist in the Atlantic Alliance than to state unequivocally if there is a 'crisis' in the relationship. 'Pacifism' is not the problem, if by that term one means a fundamental rejection of the military and all aspects of military policy. Support for the defence budget is in question, but this has been the case since the late 1960s in almost all Western democracies when the standard of comparison is the *relative priority* of defence spending to other government programmes.

Nor does 'neutralism' or 'unilateralism' truly capture the essence of public opinion. In Western Europe, support for membership of NATO remains high in all countries. In the United States, support for the commitment of troops to Western Europe remained at about 60% throughout 1982, despite the many transatlantic quarrels of the immediately preceding period. Also in the United States, support for using troops to defend Western Europe is well above its historical average of about 50%. The level of these figures may or may not be reassuring, but they are not substantially different from previous years.

In European opinion, the most noticeable change has occurred in the general image of the United States and in confidence in the wisdom of American policy. (For its part, American opinion is disappointed with the support of the allies on such questions as the Polish situation.) Further, when surveys go beyond the question of membership in NATO or alignment with the United States, respondents tend to be cautious: in most West European countries they prefer to steer clear of US–Soviet disputes.[8]

It is hardly surprising that public opinion shows most noticeable change in reaction to the question of American actions. After all, governments and scholars have for years stressed the crucial role of the United States in defining European security options and influencing the ultimate direction of policy. In a recent study of European 'influentials', there was near unanimity that the future of the Alliance depended in large part on American actions.[9] In this connection, one must once again raise the question of who is leading whom. The repeated calls for American 'leadership' and 'consistency' during the late 1970s and early 1980s came from governments and civil servants — not from public opinion. In the United States, one could argue that Mansfield-type initiatives for the reduction of US troop levels in Europe have their origins in Congressional (and Pentagon) budgetary battles rather than in mass public opinion regarding the commitment to Europe.

The economic and political interests of the United States and Europe have certainly changed over the past thirty years, but are basic attitudes towards security, arguably the most important pillar of Atlantic cooperation, also drifting apart?

Our review does not suggest any such fundamental shift. Americans have doubts that are very similar to those of West Europeans. They too dislike nuclear weapons, and they revolt at talk of *using* them. Like Europeans, Americans prefer civilian (and welfare) spending to spending on defence. True, American opinion is prone to wider swings in response to real or imagined threats, but one could argue that such swings are almost part of a periodic transatlantic learning process, the basics of which are now well-known, if no less irritating for that.

But if the basics of opinion have changed only little, the circumstances in which they will be interpreted have changed drastically. Disagreements about nuclear weapons are nothing new to the Alliance; indeed, they have preoccupied NATO planners for years. But the present round of debate occurs in a vastly different strategic situation, with the emergence of US–Soviet parity and disagreement (not just across the Atlantic) on its political implications. Similarly, debates about defence spending and burden-sharing are hardly novel. Yet the current situation is fundamentally different because it occurs at a time when specifically economic differences between the United States and Europe are intensifying. The European economy is now a strong competitor with the American, and the very interdependence which promoted that strength is also the cause of frequent rankling, as monetary policy or trade policy pursued on one side of the Atlantic generates unwelcome repercussions on the other. This change in the economic balance is probably most difficult for Americans, since it means both economic competition and loss of leverage to influence broader security policies.

These thoughts lead naturally to the conclusion that the Alliance, if not in fundamental crisis, needs to adjust to a new situation, arising from changing circumstances rather than changes in public opinion. Clearly, the United States may have to deal with a more 'Gaullist' Europe;[10] and, as suggested by a team of foreign affairs experts, Europe will have to accept increasing responsibility along with a louder voice.[11]

These concerns, however, have yet to be reflected in public opinion surveys. The polls continue to indicate considerable support for the principles upon which the Atlantic Alliance is based. To the extent that they reveal any differences among the partners, they are probably just the outcome of the evolution of arrangements which have now lasted for almost thirty-five years.

The lack of substantial change in attitudes was borne out by the recent West German and British elections. But it would be too comforting, if not complacent, to assume that policy-makers have nothing whatsoever to worry about so far as public opinion is concerned. This paper has not dealt in any detail either with the formation of public opinion or with the way in which public opinion influences policy.

If, however, one assumes that public opinion lags behind or responds to the views expressed by political leaders, then current differences between Alliance governments over the issues discussed in this paper may soon be reflected in the public's consciousness. The realization that American and European economic interests are diverging and may continue to do so as the recession deepens; different perceptions of the Soviet threat and the appropriate response; and the desire for European autonomy from America's global interests and policies now dominate the thinking in official circles and among those who participate in foreign policy and defence debates. They could produce in future the kind of changes in attitude which are currently only assumed to have taken place. This study has revealed a substantial continuity in public attitudes towards defence throughout the Alliance. It would, however, be foolhardy to assume that this will inevitably continue in the changing circumstances of the last decades of the twentieth century.

Notes

Chapter 1

1 For a discussion of the current state of the Alliance, see Eliot A.
  Cohen, 'The Long-Term Crisis of the Alliance', *Foreign Affairs*,
  Winter 1982/3, pp. 325–43. Also, Stanley Hoffman, 'NATO at
  Thirty: Variations on Old Themes', *International Security*, Summer
  1979, pp. 88–107; Alun Chalfont, 'Stormy Atlantic Weather',
  Encounter, vol. 9, no. 1 (1983), pp. 9–16; and, on the specific issue
  of burden-sharing, Simon Lunn, *Burden-sharing in NATO*, Chatham
  House Paper 18 (London, Routledge & Kegan Paul for the Royal
  Institute of International Affairs, 1983).
2 For a study of these groups and their views in the United Kingdom,
  see Peter Foot, *The Protestors*, Centrepiece 4 (Aberdeen, Centre
  for Defence Studies, 1983), passim.
3 In the United Kingdom, for example, the views of the former Chief
  of the Defence Staff, Field Marshal Lord Carver, are often cited
  by the anti-nuclear lobby.
4 Divisions over defence policy in general, and nuclear policy in
  particular, exist within both the West German Social Democratic
  and the British Labour Parties. Divisions over defence policy have
  also been evident even within the normally cohesive and outwardly
  united British Conservative Party. Witness the debates and even
  one ministerial sacking, that of Navy Minister Keith Speed, during
  Sir John Nott's tenure at the Ministry of Defence.
5 See, for example, Michael Howard, 'Reassurance and Deterrence:
  Western Defence in the 1980s', *Foreign Affairs*, Winter 1982/3,
  pp. 309–24.
6 For a brief overview of the attitudes of the various Western European countries towards INF, see Bridget Bloom, 'A Guide to
  Europe's Missile Controversy', *Financial Times*, 27 January 1983.

Chapter 2

1 V. O. Key, *Public Opinion and American Democracy* (New York, Knopf, 1961), p. 14.
2 A. Marwick, *The Explosion of British Society 1914-70* (London, Macmillan, 1971), p. 90.
3 'A Growing Peace', *Newsweek*, 24 August 1981.
4 There is the British Atlantic Committee, which exists to lobby on behalf of NATO, and the recently formed all-party campaign for a 'Home Defence Force', which would mobilize hundreds of thousands of volunteers trained to augment the United Kingdom's reserves in wartime. If it were to gain government backing, and there is little indication that it will, the Force would obviously constitute a powerful pro-defence lobby.
5 F. Teer and J. D. Spence, *Political Opinion Polls* (London, Hutchinson, 1973), p. 11.
6 B. C. Blinkley, 'The Concept of Public Opinion in the Social Sciences', in *Social Forces*, vol. 6, pp. 389-96.
7 N. Webb and R. Wybrow, *The Gallup Report* (London, Sphere, 1981), pp. 155-61.
8 Ibid.
9 According to Webb and Wybrow (ibid., p. 159), there are various alternative ways of producing a scientifically selected sample of individuals for surveys. They nearly all have in common the fact that they are constructed in at least two stages. The first stage, in Gallup's case, consists of the selection of a number of sampling points which are spread all over the country in proportion to the population in the twelve administrative regions and, within those, according to the degree of urbanization of districts, from the metropolitan areas down to rural ones. At each sample point chosen, the methodology can vary to some extent from choosing voters from the electoral register, via what is known as a random walk process (for instance, interviewing at every tenth address), to Gallup's well-known and established quota method. Gallup interviewers have strict quotas, which means that they must obtain, in a sample of ten people, a required number of men and women, of different age groups, of different social classes, and in employment or not. (These quotas are interrelated.)

Chapter 3

1 Howard, op. cit.
2 See, for example, *Gallup Political Index*, no. 234, February 1980, p. 15.
3 *Gallup Political Index*, no. 259, March 1982, p. 23.
4 *Gallup Political Index*, no. 270, February 1983, p. 15.

5 National Opinion Polls, *Political, Social and Economic Review*, no. 24, 1980, p. 8.
6 See David Capitanchik, *The Changing Attitude to Defence in Britain*, Centrepiece 2 (Aberdeen, Centre for Defence Studies, 1982), pp. 4–11.
7 See, for example, *Gallup Political Index*, no. 239, July 1980, p. 6.
8 *Gallup Political Index*, no. 263, July 1982, p. 19.
9 MORI quoted in *The Economist*, 26 June 1982.
10 An excellent account of the debate within the Church of England and also within the Scottish Churches is to be found in John Dale and Jack Webster, 'The Church and the Bomb', *Sunday Standard*, 13 February 1983, p. 15.
11 See *Gallup Political Index*, no. 214, May 1978, p. 18, and no. 253, September 1981, p. 12.
12 Polls in 1960–1, prior to the disruptive activities of the Committee of 100, showed that over 40% favoured the ideals of CND.
13 *Gallup Political Index*, no. 270, February 1983, p. 18.
14 Ibid.
15 See D. Lipsey, 'What Do We Think About the Nuclear Threat?', *New Society*, 25 September 1980.
16 *Gallup Political Index*, no. 270, loc. cit.
17 Ibid.
18 Ibid.
19 *Gallup Political Index*, no. 248, April 1981, p. 14.
20 *Gallup Political Index*, no. 299, March 1982, pp. 19–23.
21 Lipsey, op. cit.
22 See *Gallup Political Index*, no. 179, June 1975; no. 187, February 1976; no. 188, March 1976; no. 234, February 1980; and other more recent Gallup polls on Britain's position in the world.

Chapter 4

1 J. C. Voorhoeve, *Peace, Profits, Principles* (The Hague, Martinus Nijhoff, 1979), pp. 26–7.
2 This chapter is informed by conversations held by the author during August 1982 in the Hague.
3 Voorhoeve, op. cit., pp. 47–8.
4 William K. Domke, 'Conflict and Consensus: the Netherlands', in Wolf Eberwein and Catherine Kelleher, eds, *What Price Security?* (Munich, Olzog Verlag, 1983).
5 Werkgroep Kontinu-Onderzoek, FSW-A, *Dutch Continuous Survey*, Wave 9 (June/July 1975) and Wave 11 (June 1978); I am grateful to the Steinmetz Archives for showing me the results of these surveys.
6 Stichting Krijgsmacht en Maatschapij, *De Publieke Opinie over Krijgsmacht en Defensie* (The Hague, January 1982).

7   Nederlands Instituut voor de Publieke Opinie (NIPO), *Bericht*
    2188, 26 April 1982; these priorities resemble answers to the
    'most important problem' question since at least the mid-1960s.
8   Stichting Krijgsmacht en Maatschapij, op. cit.
9   NIPO, *Bericht* 2065, July 1980; Kenneth Adler and Douglas
    Wertman, 'Is NATO in Trouble?', paper presented to the 1981
    Annual Meeting of the American Association of Public Opinion
    Research, Buck Hill Falls, Pennsylvania.
10 Werkgroep Nationaal Verkiezingsonderzoek, *De Nederlandse
    Kiezer, 1967, 1972* (Alpen aan den Rijn, Samsom Uitgeverij).
11 The surveys in the preceding paragraph are from: *Nederlandse
    Kiezer, 1967*, p. 44; Inter-University Consortium for Political
    and Social Research, *Dutch Election Study, 1971* (Ann Arbor,
    Michigan, 1975), pp. 273-6; and *Dutch Continuous Survey*,
    Wave 13, November 1976. The 1980 'defence/welfare' question
    is from *Dutch Continuous Survey*, Wave 21, April 1980.
12 This section draws heavily on the work of Professor Philip Everts,
    who has reviewed and analysed the wealth of Dutch opinion
    surveys on this topic. See Everts, 'Wat denken de mensen in het
    land?' *Acta Politica*, 16 (1981), 305-54; and id., 'The Mood of
    the Country: New Data on Public Opinion in the Netherlands
    on Nuclear Weapons and Other Problems of Peace and Security',
    Acta Politica (forthcoming).
13 Id., 'The Mood of the Country', pp. 18-19.
14 NIPO, *Bericht* 2107, September 1979; NIPO, Report no. A-407/42
    (October 1979), pp. 6, 9; Everts, 'The Mood of the Country',
    pp. 18-19.
15 NIPO, Report no. A-407/42 (October 1979), p. 7.
16 *Nederlandse Kiezer*, 1971, p. 6: G. A. Irwin *et al.*, *De Nederlandse
    Kiezer '77* (Voorschoten, VAM, 1978), p. 122.
17 Adler and Wertman, op. cit; Stichting Krijgsmacht en Maatschapij,
    De Publieke Opinie.
18 Stichting Krijgsmacht en Maatschapij, op. cit.
19 US International Communications Agency, 'US Standing in West
    European Public Opinion – Some Long-term Trends', Report
    R-13-82 (July 1982), p. 8.
20 See, for example, A. W. De Porte, *Europe Between the Super-
    powers* (New Haven, Yale University Press, 1979).
21 Domke, op. cit.

Chapter 5

1   I am indebted to the writings of Johan Jørgen Holst of the Nor-
    wegian Institute of International Affairs, Oslo, for the ideas upon
    which this necessarily brief account is based – see 'Norwegian
    Security Policy for the 1980s', *Cooperation and Conflict*, vol.

17, no. 4 (1982) – and also to my colleague Dr Clive Archer for his help.

2 Again I must thank Dr Clive Archer for discussing these questions with me.

3 Holst, loc. cit., p. 222.

4 DDA-552 Gallup Omnibus Data 1980, Omnibus No. 14, August 1980.

5 DDA-552 Gallup Omnibus Data 1980, Omnibus No. 18, September 1980.

6 DDA-552 Gallup Omnibus Data 1980, Omnibus No. 22, November 1980.

7 Holst, loc. cit., p. 231.

8 Thorbjorn Grindhaug, Terje Sande og Kirsen Voje, *Galluparkivet 1964-1976* (Bergen, Norsk Samfunnsvitenskapelig Datajeneste, 1979), p. 131.

9 DDA-552 Gallup Omnibus Data 1980, Omnibus No. 15, August 1980.

10 DDA-552 Gallup Omnibus Data 1980, Omnibus No. 18, September 1980.

11 See Bertel Heurlin, 'Danish Security Policy', *Cooperation and Conflict*, vol. 17, no. 4, pp. 237-55.

12 Holst, loc. cit.

13 Ibid.

14 DDA-552 Gallup Omnibus Data 1980, Omnibus No. 2, January 1980.

Chapter 6

1 Alfred Grosser, *The Western Alliance* (London and New York, Macmillan and Random House, 1980), p. 183.

2 Pierre Saint Macary, 'Public Opinion, Defence and Armed Forces in France, 1975-1980', *Forum International*, vol. 1 (SOWI, Munich, 1982), pp. 41-80.

3 'Baromètre de l'Economie, Q.12', *L'Economie*, 19 April 1982, p. 26.

4 'L'Occident pessimiste' (Sondage Gallup-International/*L'Express*), *L'Express*, 31 December 1982 to 6 January 1983.

5 'Pour 63% des français, l'URSS est une menace', *Paris Match*, 5 February 1982.

6 George H. Gallup, ed., *The Gallup International Public Opinion Polls*, vol. 2, *France, 1968-75* (New York, Random House, 1979).

7 *L'Express* (as n. 4).

8 *Ça m'intéresse*, October 1982, pp. 66-7.

9 *Le Matin*, 25 October 1982, pp. 18-19.

10 Louis Harris, *La Vie*, 18 November 1982, pp. 26-31.

11 Macary, loc. cit., p. 72.

12 Harris, loc. cit., p. 29.
13 *Paris Match* (as n. 5), p. 81.
14 *Ça m'intéresse*, p. 66.
15 Macary, loc. cit., pp. 72–3.
16 Jacqueline Grapin, 'Alliance atlantique: fidélité à l'union libre', *Le Point*, 15 March 1982.
17 See Grosser, op. cit.
18 Grapin, loc. cit.
19 See Chapter 3 above.
20 *Ça m'intéresse*, p. 67.
21 *Paris Match* (as n. 5).

Chapter 7

1 The rearmament phase is discussed in Reinhard Mutz, *Sicherheitspolitik und demokratische Oeffentlichkeit in der BRD* (Munich, Oldenbourg Verlag, 1978).
2 Ibid., p. 101.
3 The survey question asked: 'By and large, do you have a good opinion or not a good opinion of the Bundeswehr?' The surveys are reprinted in E. P. Neumann and Elisabeth Noelle-Neumann, *Jahrbuch der Oeffentlichen Meinung*, vol. 5, 1968–73 (Munich, Verlag Fritz Molden, 1976), and Allensbacher Institut für Demoskopie, *Allensbacher Berichte*, vol. 31, no. 1 (1980), p. 4.
4 These results are based on a question posed to males only, which asked if the response to a draft call would be met 'gladly', 'as a necessary duty', or 'only unhappily or not at all'. The percentages reported in the text refer to those responding 'gladly' or 'duty'. The surveys were provided in mimeograph form by the Press and Information Office, Federal Ministry of Defence.
5 Press and Information Office, Federal Ministry of Defence, *Hinweise für Oeffentlichkeitsarbeit*, no. 7 (1979).
6 Yearly 'threat indexes' constructed from polls for the Federal Ministry of Defence show that threat perception began increasing gradually in 1973 and reached the level of the 1960s once again in 1976.
7 In May 1979, 29% were 'very' or 'fairly' concerned about a Soviet military attack; in March 1981, the figure was 31%. See Kenneth Adler and Douglas Wertman, 'Is NATO in Trouble'?, paper delivered to the 1981 Annual Meeting of the American Association of Public Opinion Research, Buck Hill Falls, Pennsylvania.
8 Similar priorities are revealed in yearly 'most important problem' surveys. See Kendal Baker, Russell Dalton and Kai Kildebrandt, *German Politics Transformed* (Cambridge, Harvard University Press, 1981).
9 Hans D. Klingemann and Charles Lewis Taylor, 'Partisanship,

Candidates and Issues: Attitudinal Components of the Vote in West German Federal Elections', in Max Kaase and Klaus von Beymen, eds, *Elections and Parties* (Beverly Hills, Sage Publications, 1978). This study extends only to the 1976 election.

10 Polls on the military balance are published in: Adler and Wertman, 'NATO'; Neumann and Noelle-Neumann, *Jahrbuch*; and in Press and Information Office, *Hinweise*.

11 Similar priorities were revealed in polls conducted between 1975 and 1978.

12 EMNID Institute, *EMNID Informationen*, vol. 39, no. 2-3 (1981); the second poll is from *Der Spiegel*, no. 48 (23 November 1981), p. 59.

13 'Breite Mehrheit', *Capital*, no. 8 (1981), p. 88.

14 'Breite Mehrheit', p. 88 (italics ours).

15 *Der Spiegel*, p. 59.

16 'Breite Mehrheit', p. 88.

17 Neumann and Noelle-Neumann, op. cit., p. 535; *The Economist*, 27 February 1982.

18 Office of Research, US International Communications Agency, 'US Standing in West European Public Opinion — Some Long-term Trends', July 1982, mimeographed.

19 'Breite Mehrheit', p. 90.

20 Office of Research, US International Communications Agency, 'A Profile of West European Neutralism', 28 October 1981, mimeographed.

21 Stephen Szabo, 'Generations and Changing Security Perspectives in West Germany' (Washington, Foreign Service Institute, 1982), mimeographed.

22 The well-known exception concerning generational change in general is Ronald Inglehart, *The Silent Revolution* (Princeton, Princeton University Press, 1977). See also Baker *et al.*, *German Politics Transformed*.

23 Office of Research, US International Communications Agency, 'A Profile of West European "Nuclear Pacifism"', 28 January 1982, mimeographed.

24 Of course, a significant impact can occur when a minority occupies a swing role in coalition negotiations. In the past, this has not caused undue concern owing to the moderate tone of the Free Democrats, but it may lead to problems with the entry of the neutralist Greens into the Bundestag.

Chapter 8

1 Daniel Yankelovich and Larry Kaagan, 'Assertive America', *Foreign Affairs*, vol. 59, no. 3 (America and the World, 1980), p. 696.

2 Ellen Malone and Alvin Richman, 'American Attitudes Toward

the Building and Use of Military Power', materials presented to the Convention of the International Studies Association, Cincinnati, Ohio, March 1982; the poll cited is from Roper.

3 The Reagan programme and the public's reaction is described in great detail in 'Reagan und die Sicherheit des Westens', in Wolf-Dieter Eberwein and Catherine Kelleher, eds, *Sicherheit zu Welchem Preis?* (Munich, Olzog Verlag, 1983).

4 'A Conversation with Louis Harris', *Bulletin of the Atomic Scientist*, August/September 1982, p. 4.

5 Malone and Richman, op. cit., p. 2.

6 'A Conversation with Louis Harris', p. 4.

7 Lloyd A. Free and William Watts, 'Internationalism Comes of Age . . . Again', *Public Opinion*, vol. 3, no. 2 (1980), p. 49.

8 The figures on the use of troops to defend West Europe were provided by the Chicago Council on Foreign Relations from their recent poll (by Gallup) on American opinion on foreign policy. See also *World Opinion Update*, vol. 4, no. 2 (1980), p. 52.

9 Alvin Richman, 'Public Attitudes on Military Power', *Public Opinion*, vol. 4, no. 6 (1982), p. 46.

10 Ibid.

11 Ibid. It is significant that broader studies of American public opinion find that the old 'isolationist/internationalist' cleavage has been replaced by a new opinion structure in which 'forceful internationalists' and 'cooperative internationalists' are distinguished from isolationists; see Eugene Wittkopf, 'The Structure of Foreign Policy Attitudes', *Social Science Quarterly*, 62 (March 1981), pp. 108-23.

12 Caspar Weinberger, *Report of the Secretary of Defense to the Congress on FY 1983 Budget and FY 1984 Authorization Request and FY 1983-1987 Defense Programs* (Washington, Department of Defense, 1982), p. I-1.

13 The 65% figure is from an NBC/*Washington Post* survey reported in Malone and Richman, op. cit., pp. 6-7.

14 *Public Opinion*, vol. 8, no. 9 (1979), p. 17; and *Public Opinion*, vol. 12, no. 1 (1980), p. 40.

15 Polls by ABC/*Washington Post*, January, March and April 1982 press releases.

16 *New York Times*, 6 February 1983, p. 1.

17 Louis Harris, 'Americans Want Nuclear Arms Reduction', *World Opinion Update*, vol. 7, no. 8 (1982), p. 90.

18 Malone and Richman, 'American Attitudes', p. 9.

19 NBC/*Washington Post*, press release dated 25 October 1982; 'A Conversation with Louis Harris', p. 3; Harris, 'Americans Want', p. 90.

20 'A Conversation with Louis Harris', pp. 3-4; and unpublished survey results by Cambridge Associates, May 1982.

Chapter 9

1 See: Seyom Brown, *New Forces in World Politics* (Washington, Brookings Institution, 1974); Edward Morse, *Foreign Policy and Interdependence in Gaullist France* (Princeton, Princeton University Press, 1974); and Robert Keohane and Joseph Nye, *Power and Interdependence* (Boston, Little, Brown, 1977).

2 Arthur F. Burns, 'How America Looks at Europe', speech delivered in Bonn, 1 September 1981, printed in *American Enterprise Institute Defense and Foreign Policy Review*, 3/6 (1982), pp. 1-5; Francis Pym, 'Defense in Democracies: The Public Dimension', *International Security*, 7/1 (Summer 1982), pp. 40-4; and Hans-Dietrich Genscher, 'The Spiritual Foundations of German-American Friendship', speech delivered at Würtzburg University, 13 January 1983, as translated and printed in *The German Tribune Political Affairs Review*, 20 February 1983, pp. 21-3.

3 Ronald Inglehart, *The Silent Revolution* (Princeton, Princeton University Press, 1975).

4 Compare the comments on the 'American model' in the contributions to the special edition of *Daedalus* (Winter 1964) with those from earlier periods in Grosser, *The Western Alliance*.

5 Harold and Margaret Sprout, 'The Dilemma of Declining Resources and Rising Demands', *World Politics*, vol. 20 (1968), pp. 660-93; and Morse, *Foreign Policy and Interdependence*. See also the many writings of David Greenwood on the evolution of British defence and social priorities.

6 Peter Flora, 'The Welfare State: The Problem or the Solution?', in W. J. Mommsen, ed., *The Emergence of the Welfare State in Britain and Germany* (London, Croom Helm, 1981).

7 The meaning of this question is somewhat obscured by the reference to Western Europe in a survey that includes questions on a wide variety of topics relating to regional integration. None the less, the question is identical for all countries, and the reference to 'strengthening' probably means that the question taps the notion of increasing spending.

8 A poll in March 1980 asked if governments should 'back the US against the Soviet Union more than it has until now' or 'do everything possible to stay out of arguments' between the two countries. The percentages preferring to 'stay out of arguments' were 37% (West Germany), 66% (France) and 55% (Britain). See *Washington Post*, 17 April 1980.

9 See the concluding chapter by Catherine Kelleher in Eberwein and Kelleher, eds, op. cit.

10 See the article by Fritz Stern, 'Germany in a Semi-Gaullist Europe', *Foreign Affairs*, vol. 58, no. 4 (1980), pp. 867-86.

11 Karl Kaiser, *et al.*, *Western Security: What Has Changed? What Should be Done?* (London, Royal Institute of International Affairs, 1981).

Chatham House Papers

Chatham House Papers provide full and up-to-date information on major issues of foreign policy, together with expert analysis. They are recognized as valuable and authoritative guides to some of the most important policy debates of the day. An annual subscription to six papers costs £22.00. We list current and forthcoming titles overleaf. If you would like to subscribe, please complete the form below.

SUBSCRIPTION ORDER FORM

Please return this form to:

Subscriptions,
Routledge & Kegan Paul,
Broadway House,
Newtown Road,
Henley-on-Thames,
Oxon RG9 1EN, England

or in USA or Canada to:

Subscriptions,
Routledge & Kegan Paul,
9 Park Street,
Boston,
MA 02108, USA

Please enter a subscription to Chatham House Papers (£22.00)

I enclose a cheque for_____
Please charge my Access/Barclaycard Number_____

Signature_____
Name_____
      (BLOCK CAPITALS)

Address _____
_____
_____

Chatham House Papers